The Secret
SUCCESSI
COPYWRITING

C000156134

About the author

Born forty-eight years ago in the East End of London, Patrick Quinn originally trained as a compositor. But National Service brought him into fortunate contact with the Forces Broadcasting Service in North Africa — for whom he compiled and presented record programmes.

Back in civvy street, he was soon scripting radio plays and writing what he describes as excruciating detective novels.

Armed with all of this published (and unpublished) material, he 'won' his way into a copywriting job with a Bond Street advertising agency. This was largely accomplished by studiously losing to the copy chief in a game of poker dice.

Twenty-five years on, via agencies in Dublin, the USA and Scotland, he has won for his clients just about every advertising award worth winning — including a Grand Prix at the Cork International Film Festival.

The holder of a Private Pilots Licence, and a keen flyer, his remaining ambition is to inherit a brewery.

Books in the series

The Secrets of
SUCCESSFUL
COPYWRITING

Patrick Quinn

Heinemann Professional Publishing

For Marion, of course

Heinemann Professional Publishing Ltd
22 Bedford Square, London WC1B 3HH

LONDON   MELBOURNE   AUCKLAND

First published 1986
First published as a paperback edition 1988

© Patrick Quinn 1986

British Library Cataloguing in Publication Data
Quinn, Patrick
   The secrets of successful copywriting.
   1. Advertising copy
   I. Title
   659.13'22   HF5825

ISBN 0 434 91611 0 cased
      0 434 91613 7 paper

Set in 11/13 Baskerville by Deltatype, Ellesmere Port
Printed in Great Britain by Billing & Sons Ltd, Worcester

Contents

Foreword

I don't know that I agree with everything that Patrick Quinn has written in the following pages.

What I do know is that it needed to be written.

Back in the days when I became a copywriter, when dinosaurs roamed the earth, there were no copywriting colleges, no 'How to' books, and no great understanding of what copywriting actually was. Lord Peter Wimsey did it, I seem to remember in *Murder Must Advertise*, and Clark Gable had written radio ads for beauty soap in a forties movie called *The Hucksters*. I actually believed I was applying for a job as a copy *typist* when I stumbled into advertising (and sat for two days wondering why nobody gave me anything to type).

I don't know if it was easier getting into advertising in those days. In retrospect nobody really seemed to be choosing it as a career. More as a bridging period before they (a) got their novel published or (b) decided what they really wanted to do in life.

At least today copywriting is a career. People take it seriously. I know. I get fifteen or twenty letters a week from youngsters who are desperate to get into advertising. Into copywriting, in particular.

In his first chapter, Patrick Quinn says that he can't teach you how to write. I'd amend that slightly. Nobody can teach you how to think. And above all you need to be able to think. If you have a modicum of writing talent you can pick up the tricks of the trade – and by the time you've finished this book, you'll know quite a few of them.

That thinking doesn't just refer to thinking about the specific brief in hand. It's an ability to take on a problem and think about it differently – laterally is the chic term at the moment. All it means is to look at something in a way no one has before. I remember that when I was a very young writer at Pritchard Wood & Partners (you probably won't have heard of it, but you may know of three of its alumni: Martin Boase, Stanley Pollitt, Gabe Massimi), an art director was hired solely on the fact that he had mentioned in passing that a cow, if looked at from above, is the same shape as a violin. That's lateral thinking; and if you can bring it to the copy you write, you can't fail.

One final point. If this book works the way you want it to work, I guess I'll be hearing about you. Very soon.

Don White
Executive Creative Director, McCann-Erickson Limited
(Committee Member – The Advertising Creative Circle)

Preface

Like Lady Bracknell, I have never really approved of anything that tampers with natural ignorance. Thus, teaching people how to write better copy is not an occupation I have consciously adopted. Rather, it has adopted me.

Allow me to explain.

My office postbag regularly contains letters from a lot of anxious people wanting to know how to get into the advertising business. More correctly, they want to know how to get into copywriting.

I answer the lot.

I also receive phone calls. Dozens of them. The calls I am talking about usually originate from people who are, in one way or another, already in advertising. They may be employed in an industrial company's publicity department; they may be eager-beaver visualizers and designers; or they may be up-and-coming sales-promotion/marketing executives. Whatever the case, they come on with myriad requests. They casually ask for formulas which will improve their headline-writing skills; for definitions of technical terms to do with radio and television commercial scripting; for considered opinions on mailing-shots they have cobbled together; and for off-the-cuff pointers on how to distil fifty words of pertinent copy from a written briefing-sheet that contains five hundred.

Just recently, I spent an hour on the phone with a careers officer of a local college. She needed the basic why's and wherefore's of copywriting to pass on to her students. It so happens that the older I become, the more I tend to relate to women. Sadly, though, the older I become, increasingly fewer women seem prepared to relate to me. So when this siren-voiced charmer requested the facts, how could I possibly refuse? As I say, it took an hour to transmit the bare essentials.

Teaching, as you can therefore see, has been studiously thrust upon me.

Now it follows that all this time spent replying to correspondence and chatting on phones isn't spent doing what I should be doing. Writing copy. And I learned long ago that what you don't write you don't get paid for.

Assuming the role of guru is fine when your audience is liberally sprinkled with wealthy pop-stars prepared to invest large sums for the doubtful privilege of sitting at one's feet. Unhappily, the vast majority of people who contact me are neither wealthy nor pop-stars. I would even go so far as to say that the great bulk of them are completely broke and very likely couldn't hold a note in a bucket.

Nevertheless, it is not lost on me that someone way back took the trouble to put me on the right road – a Herculean labour for which I am eternally grateful, since writing copy beats working any day of the week. Sadly, Henry Stephen Baker is no longer with us. Though I am prepared to bet that he is currently installed in the great copy shop in the sky, perhaps demonstrating to the board exactly how certain stone tablets can readily be condensed to five with no appreciable loss of emphasis or urgency. That being the case, I suppose it falls to me to do the right and proper thing and pass on what I know about advertising in general and copywriting in particular to those who want to know it.

There lies the purpose of this book. It's for those thinking of joining the profession and who wish to grasp the fundamentals. And it's for those already ensconced, but who are prepared to admit that, like the rest of us, they don't know it all and might just pick up a wrinkle or two.

I apologize in advance to the latter if some of the material herein appears a touch patronizing, or a shade elementary. In its defence, I would say only that we each had to start somewhere; so rock bottom is where we start here. I will also be the first to admit that none of my headline/copy examples are in any respect deathless. I'll confess to good, but not imperishable.

With any luck, this volume will also give some pause to all those letter-writers and phone-callers. But if you feel you simply have to (here we go again), do drop me a line.

I also apologize in advance to lady readers for the constant use of the male gender throughout this book. The word 'man' has been used to mean man or woman and its use does not imply that women are not as effective as men. In my experience women are as competent as men ever knew how to be – and sometimes more so

Patrick Quinn

Acknowledgements

A good many people have been involved in the preparation of this book. Some I know personally – others I don't. But whichever the case, I thank each one unreservedly.

My eternal gratitude is due to 'Joe' Baker – unquestionably the cleverest copywriter of them all. And my appreciation is given to the following ad agencies for allowing me to reproduce samples of their work:

J. Walter Thompson, London
Covey Advertising, Edinburgh
Geers Gross, London
Bill Hopkins and Joe Baker, London
Halls Advertising, Edinburgh
Allen, Brady & Marsh, London
McCann–Erickson, London

Apologies, too, to those who also submitted examples of good advertising, but which, solely for reasons of space, could not be included.

Most importantly, my sincere thanks to Marion – secretary, co-pilot, typist, navigator, sympathetic ear, wife, and remarkable lady.

1   The copywriter

The craft of copywriting demands an agile brain, a wide general knowledge, a high IQ and so intimate an understanding of the Queen's English that one can abuse it with impunity.

A word, first of all, about the copywriter and about his place in the advertising business. And while this section is addressed primarily to the writer in the making, I believe that everyone who puts pen to paper in order to help shift product – from advertising managers to account-handlers – should derive some benefit from it. Even if it's only the satisfaction of disagreeing violently with everything I say.

The quotation at the head of this chapter implies that copywriters are endowed with a reasonably high standard of education which, in its turn, usually implies a reasonably up-market background. The proposition is largely true; any exceptions to the general rule – and there are plenty – are those who have worked like stink and pulled themselves up by their bootstraps. So although they have little in the way of certificated academic prowess, they are well above average when it comes to the use of words.

But it's also true to say that the vast majority of products, whether industrial or consumer, are not sold to people of this type or with this background. They are sold to people with few pretentions to higher education and who wouldn't recognize a literary allusion if it leapt up and announced itself. Where the copywriter is literate, they have little or no interest in syntax or grammar; where he is imaginative, they are earthy; where he is enthusiastic, they are indifferent. This is the great schism.

There are a few, a happy few, who can bridge the gap with the adroitness of Mr Bailey. And being rare, they are expensive. Apart from them, the copywriter ranks are filled by four main types:

The mediocre   Those whose work is undistinguished, but mostly unexceptionable. There's nothing specifically good about their work, but nothing particularly wrong with it either.

The effulgent   Those to whom ideas come easily and who can improvize with words and thoughts as readily as a latter-day Byron. They can be truly valuable – sometimes invaluable; but they are no one's backbone. And all too often they are dilettanti incapable, as the actress said, of hard, grinding, unflagging effort.

The undeserving   Those who have drifted into advertising and who can't drift out again soon enough for me. They tend to think of the whole thing as a bit of a chuckle and really rather beneath them. They are in advertising not because they like it or believe in it, but as a way of making a little dishonest money until Radio Four starts accepting their plays – which it seldom does.

The grafters   Those who view the business as a worthwhile career, and one that gives them the opportunity to spend their lives doing something they enjoy: selling through writing. They are the mainstay of advertising and while they rarely win acclaim, to say nothing of awards, their work is consistently competent. This kind will attack a brochure for a small, micro-engineering outfit with the same enthusiasm as they'd fetch to a six-commercial, national TV campaign for Cadbury or BL. They are an asset to their agency and a credit to themselves.

It has been said by others, and I agree, that too many copywriters have far too little ability and far too high an opinion of their artistic talents. Really good writers are scarcer than cabs on a wet night, and even the grafters mentioned above don't come easy. Ask any agency copy chief.

What initial advice, then, have I to offer potential copywriters? Just this. If you are as good as you fancy you are, you will have (or should have) no trouble imposing yourself upon your agency executives and your clients. They should come to think so highly of your work that they are always afraid you will sulk and withdraw your services. If they don't, then maybe you are not a very good copywriter after all.

But if you insist on pursuing the occupation of copywriter and find yourself behind an agency desk, take the opportunity in both hands. Don't meddle. Don't get involved in politics. Push your talent rather than yourself. Take the rough with the smooth and be grateful – be very grateful – that you are probably getting more of the smooth than the rough.

Maybe I should explain.

During my twenty-odd years in the advertising business, I've learned how ninety per cent of a copywriter's life is spent proving to anyone who will listen that during the other ten per cent of the time he *can* actually write. If and when you join an advertising agency, you will discover that most of your best ideas never leave the building; they will be bucketed with a regularity to make your head spin. What's even worse, those creative ideas which do see the light of day will, largely, be accredited to someone else – usually the person who looks after the account: the account director.

Advertising is, in every respect, uncompromising; it can reduce strong men to tears and it can turn the even stronger gender to booze and promiscuity overnight. Setting aside evenings for a few rounds of solitary Russian-roulette should, by comparison, be considered a pretty ordinary way of life.

But the first and overriding principle of advertising – and one you must have firmly implanted in your mind – is that advertising is all about selling. All about shifting product: whether that product be seats on multimillion pound airlines or a tu'penny-ha'penny tube of sweets. Thus, if you've any aversion to the profit motive, or if the word profit leaves you with a nasty taste, you are most definitely backing the wrong horse. Fortunately for all of us, the copywriter doesn't have to sell himself the way the average salesperson does. Face to face. We do it behind the scenes on paper and are, therefore, anonymously and thankfully hidden from a cold, hard world that isn't noticeably falling over itself to buy our stuff. Additionally, whatever personal reservations you may have about it, the product is always king. At least, it always is when you are within earshot of the client. After all, he believes that whatever he manufactures is the greatest thing to happen since reptiles crawled out of the swamps; and because he is going a good way to paying your wages, you'd jollywell better think the same way.

Nearly finally, advertising has changed more than somewhat in the last ten years or so. In the main it is researched, calculated, response-planned and generally anticepticized to a point where good old gut feeling and common sense plays little part. That's what they'd like to think anyway. In reality, it still comes down to a couple of blokes, or ladies, just like you and me turning their brains inside out in an effort to say something different about a product they have said something different about every three months for the past five years.

We will, of course, discuss the value of research at a later moment. For the time being, however, lets close this item on the writer proper with a deck-clearing exercise.

I cannot, under any circumstances, teach you to write. You either can, or you can't. You'll know yourself whether it's the former by the way you continue to submit manu-scripts for publication despite several million previous rejections. You'll know by the way you everlastingly criticize what you see written all around you – not only advertising, but also TV programmes, magazine articles, newspaper features and so on. And, not to put too fine a point on it, you wouldn't be reading this book unless you had a sneaking feeling that with a little encouragement you could write the rest of us out of the park. Well, would you?

What I can teach you, however, is this. 1 The principles of copywriting. 2 The art of refining a complicated brief into a simple selling message. 3 The techniques for developing ideas. 4 The nuts and bolts of radio and television work.

And this I propose to do.

Later, we'll discuss peripheral matters like the secrets of taking agency copy tests. Right now, though, a few specific thoughts about the advertising business might be in order. I include these because without a basic understanding of what makes it tick, the entire mechanics of copywriting will remain equally mysterious.

Stand by.

Rule 1 *A good copywriter has the happy knack of appearing both restrained and arrogant at one and the same time.*

2   Agencies and their clients

Advertising, as I am sure you know, helps make the money go round. It spreads the word; creates cashflow; occasions employment; and, done properly, fetches largesse.

Take a case, for instance, where a very clever chap employs five hundred people to manufacture the definitive and provably-instant cure for baldness. Let's call it Hair Today. Unless consumers begin purchasing his product in something of a hurry, he will be in trouble. With little or no revenue coming in, he'll be unable to buy more materials and unable to pay the work force. So it's on the cards that Hair Today will certainly be gone tomorrow. His business will collapse, his employees will be decanted on to the dole, and you and I won't get the benefit of a remarkable head of hair overnight. It stands to reason, then, that he must make his product known far and wide; and he must sell it far and wide via advertising. Now, where does he promote this supreme answer to every shiny-pated individual's wildest dreams? *Motorboat and Yachting*? Hardly. *Punk Weekly*? Not really. The percentage of bald readers of the latter rag may not only be somewhat small, but also genuinely uncaring. Not to go overboard on this teaching-of-grandmothers cameo, our manufacturer obviously goes to an ad agency, where they know exactly how to market the product. Furthermore, they have the personnel who can expertly select the appropriate media for the job, and also the people capable of writing, designing and illustrating his advertising in a convincing way.

To understand this more fully, we must take a look at the structure of an agency. In configuration it's like a pyramid. At the very bottom is the creative team: the writers, the visualizers, the designers and, allowably, the finished artists. If there were any justice in this world – which there patently isn't – this crew would be top dogs. After all, it's their ideas, their words and pictures which keep the rest of the pyramid gainfully employed. They aren't. So that's an end to it.

Now travel a short way up the pyramid and you arrive at the account executives. These are the people who service clients day to day. Their function is to take briefs from clients. (Notice the allusion to law, and thus the assumed respectability.) To the copywriter, a brief is an instruction on which products the client wishes to push, when and how. More properly, the brief is an interpretation of a given market in relation to the product, plus every usable detail about the features and benefits of that product. The account executive fetches this back to the agency, transmits the facts to the creative team chosen for the task and awaits their solution. Once this is provided, he returns to the client and presents the proposals.

Now you may be forgiven for thinking that the run-of-the-mill account executive is little more than a messenger, fetching and carrying between client and agency. In all certainty, you are right – but never, ever say so. Before we go one whit further, allow me to say that I have nothing against account executives – they have a rotten enough job without me making things worse by rubbing it in. I'll even go one step better and interpret some of the problems they face.

For some unfathomable reason, agencies always talk about clients instead of using the more earthy appellation of customers. Ask me why and I shall look blank – which I

don't find difficult. One answer might be that the customer is always right and, as far as agencies are concerned, the client is always wrong. Certainly, some outfits are famous for being an unyielding bunch of diggers-in of toes, impassive turners of blind eyes and deaf ears. My own experience is that the majority of agencies, including some of the biggest, don't argue with their clients half enough. They go through the motions, of course, but deep in the heart of the average agency chief is the belief, probably implanted at birth, that when it comes to the crunch the client really knows best about his advertising. It *is* his money, isn't it?

Executives as a race, therefore, have an unenviable lot; they lead a harassed and hag-ridden life, badgered and kicked from all points of the compass. They are constantly haunted by the thought of all those pre-booked spaces in publications demanding to be filled by a certain date; and constantly frustrated in the filling of them by the unreasonable demands and continuing procrastination of the clients on the one hand, and the unreasonable attitudes and continuing procrastination of the creative mob on the other. Morton's fork and Procrustes' bed had nothing on what the unhappy executive has to cope with.

Can one wonder, therefore, that he grasps at any supporting straw? Or that he doesn't feel impelled to put on the whole armour of God in defence of every ad he presents?

Copywriters and designers are a different breed. Not necessarily a more attractive breed – just different. Unleash a copywriter on an unsuspecting client and he will defend the work he's done with a power of mind that would levitate tables. There is, undoubtedly, a simple explanation for this. If the copywriter concerned is any good, he will have put into any given piece of work a little of what passes for his soul; and no one takes a man's soul away without his kicking and scratching a little.

Advertising is a funny business, because it *isn't* only a business. Advertising, I hold, is half a business, quarter a profession and quarter an art. The proportions may be debatable but the principle isn't. And it's the art bit that creative people feel strongly, possibly over-strongly, about and which clients tend to ignore.

Once, in my earshot, a client asked a designer for a few more specimens. What he meant was a few more rough layouts, or visuals. This in itself was bad enough, since the poor bloke had been up half the night producing the 'specimens' mentioned, but to hear it expressed in such jar-and-litmus-paper terms brought the designer near to apoplexy. That he didn't have to stand trial for inflicting GBH is a tribute to my own quick-wittedness. In a flash, I had forced a stiff gin down his throat and changed the subject.

Manifestly, a client should leave the creation of his advertising to the people he pays to create it; and if it doesn't get the results he's looking for all he has to do is change his agency to one that does. Were the same man to observe a dustman emptying his bin, he'd hardly be likely to call him over and suggest a more efficient way of doing the job because, in all probability, he'd shortly be wearing a half-hundredweight of refuse. Yet this is precisely the sort of treatment that copywriters and designers have to put up with all the time.

It isn't right, it isn't fair. Copywriters and designers reckon they can do their job better than anyone else – and ninety per cent of the time, they're right.

Thus, the role of the account executive in the client/agency set-up is much that of a buffer. He is the fall-guy.

But this is a function not without its value. It saves direct confrontation, personal abrasion and a whole lot of account-changing. The system is essentially pragmatic and in business terms, pragmatism wins over idealism every time.

Farther up the pyramid are account executives' bosses, the account directors. These fellows and ladies monitor the executive's work on given accounts and do their best to appear to know what's going on when they see the client for lunch four times a year. It's their job, also, to make sure that the client pays his due bills. Account directors are the agency's marketing people proper; and I have a grudging respect for them.

Onward and upward, we come to the media planners whose job it is to select the right media, i.e. the correct market-place and audience for the product we want to shift.

Media people are learned people and extremely adept at buying space and air-time at preferential rates. I know of one highly respected media man who makes more money for his agency, via wheeling and dealing, than any other ten people on the payroll. Be friends with media wallahs; they can make the copywriter's life so much easier.

Around about the middle of the pyramid come the traffic and production teams – the characters who are constantly in your hair, demanding this, that and the other to unreasonable deadlines. They chase you up, they harass, they won't stop until they get the piece of work in question; then they bustle away to shade in the blanks on their progress charts.

In a large agency, you will find intermixed with the foregoing departments, a myriad of branch functions, i.e. experts on below-the-line promotions, experts on recruitment advertising, experts on print-buying and experts who seem to do nothing in particular, but are always in evidence at management meetings. These faceless ones are invariably the hatchet men, the horsemen of the apocalypse who descend upon the unwary late on an afternoon brandishing employment cards, and termination cheques. Their war cry is often: 'Look, it's nothing to do with me, old chap. Sorry and all that. They are letting you go. Please clear your desk'.

The foregoing is no more than a general picture of agency structure. More important for our purposes is the format of the creative department itself. In larger agencies, things called creative groups are set up, meaning that a writer or two joins a visualizer or art director or two on a permanent basis to work on a parcel of accounts. Sometimes that means only one or two accounts; and it's that kind of happy situation where advertising of the superlative standard of Guinness, ICI and the like is born. Smaller agencies cannot afford such luxuries and everyone – including the tea-boy – works on everything. At the head of the department is the creative director. He will come from either the writing or the drawing disciplines; and simply because of that he may be treated as a non-belligerent. Most of the time a creative director will fight the creative team's corner with some tenacity but, understandably, this will make him unpopular elsewhere. Hence the fairly rapid turnover of the ilk throughout the business. Just beneath the creative director you may be fortunate in having a copy chief. Here's a bloke who can, if you pay attention and be ever so obsequious, teach you the complete works and put you on the train to fame. As a loose rule, copy chiefs are of an older breed; and the reason for this is that they are probably too bolshie to be made creative directors and too good to be designated ordinary copywriters. Thus, the management gets the benefits of their ability without the aggravation they would cause if elevated.

*   *   *

Advertising agencies are often accused of thinking that they have some kind of a lien on conscience; and of hawking their so-called integrity around the place with bared and beaten breasts showing through the sackcloth. This happens when an agency professes an inclination to 'turn out decent work' and when it moans (as most of them do) that it is frustrated in these intentions by the stupidity, cupidity or rank inefficiency of the client it works for.

'Why,' runs the counter argument to this, 'do agencies, particularly the self-styled creative people in them, have to run off at the mouth so much about their principles, their standards and their souls? Why can't they, like any other business, simply supply what the customer wants and be glad to take the money?'

At first sight, a reasonable argument – but it happens to be wholly fallacious. The fallacy is that most businesses don't supply what the individual customer wants, irrespective of its quality. A manufacturer of top-class hammers doesn't deliberately produce a batch of substandard tools to suit one wholesaler. A maker of videotape recorders would very properly decline to knock out a quota of them which, in his opinion, wouldn't have a hope of doing an adequate job. A whisky distiller would rather leap into the nearest loch than bottle a drop of the stuff in which he couldn't take a reasonable pride.

Sadly, in this respect, an advertising agency is out on a very rickety limb. It has no convenient, anonymous label under which to hide work that doesn't come up to par. It has to admit to every ad it produces. If an ad is bad, the agency hasn't a leg to stand on. It is bad because of creative incompetence, or executive weakness. There's no other excuse.

It's true to say that any business grows and prospers on its reputation and on the standards it sets itself. This applies to agencies as much as it does to anyone else. If, then, an agency is forced by a client into producing work which is manifestly poor or wrong in their eyes, then he is not simply misusing his own money. He's doing worse: he's ruining the agency's potential future prosperity.

Thus, agency tantrums aren't necessarily a revolt of the artist against the Philistine. Much more likely, they're the reaction of businessmen (as hard-headed in their way as anybody) against clients playing God with their reputation.

Some years ago, a well-known and well-respected American agency ran a house-ad (an ad promoting themselves) which said: '*We'd rather go out of business than create a weak advertisement*'. Their copy went on to say that their policy was to refuse to work for clients if their products didn't offer a real benefit; and to fire clients if they attempted to monkey around with what the agency conceived to be a good commercial message.

Noble sentiments; and sentiments that I applauded with great gusto. I have no idea whether they are still functioning.

If there's any natural justice at all, they certainly should be. But I doubt it. And I doubt it because their philosophy was too good to last.

As an example of how a client can bring an agency into mild disrepute, let me tell you about one agency I worked for that had a banking organization as a client.

This bank was, and still is, extremely powerful; and it had a habit of running its agency like it would run any other department of its organization; and the agency let it. The agency, you see, was frightened of losing the account, since the billing was several millions in hard, negotiable currency. So it performed, leapt through hoops and when the command came to jump, it always asked: 'How high?'

It came inevitably to pass, then, that we were given the ultimate *fait accompli* over a television campaign which was being planned. Seemingly, some bank publicity-officer or other, while on holiday in the United States, had chanced to see a television campaign for a west-coast bank – the content of which he had fallen head-over-heels in love with. This being so, he acquired a 16 mm print of the commercials and screened it for his confederates back at the bank. They, too, became smitten. So much so, they called us in for a viewing and, at the subsequent discussion, told us that after certain modifications, they wanted to re-shoot and run this campaign for themselves.

Now I don't want to do anything which might disrupt whatever is left of the Anglo-American special relationship, but advertising that is right for US audiences isn't necessarily right for British audiences. I am the first to admit that we more backward countries can learn a lot from our friends across the water. Their work is often exemplary. Yet, in this instance, the only lesson we were likely to learn was where to draw the line.

In spite of our best efforts and best arguments, the bank insisted upon using the west-coast bank theme. All we had to do was put it into the British idiom – or, in this case, idiot.

And that was the mistake of mistakes, because American humour tends not to translate too well into proper English; and the theme of the thing was all-singing, all-dancing American humour.

Anyway, we did as we were bid, though not without a struggle. While the films were being made, our creative people put together several alternative campaigns, which, in our view, were streets ahead of the material we had been lumbered with. This alternative material was presented to the bank officials by the account director and myself at a meeting I shall merely describe as tense. I admit that I lost my head somewhat at the closed-mind attitude of the client; and I made no bones about what I thought. The denouement came as my colleague was taken into an ante-room by the bank's marketing officer. They reappeared some minutes later, the account director looking for all the world as though he had been kneed in the groin; and by the way he half-inclined his head towards the door, I knew the interview was over.

The campaign ran, but it was a complete and utter disaster. And the bank, which had been claiming for years to be number one, was overtaken in weeks by number two. What's more, the agency lost the account eventually, anyway.

All of which goes to show what happens when people keep dogs but insist on barking themselves.

*   *   *

There is a final consideration about agency work which should be borne in mind. For reasons which I fully understand, but am quite unable to go along with, very many creative people seem unwilling to come to terms with the commercialism of it all. They feel that their art is somehow being sold down the river, calculated as it is in implacable pounds and pence.

All I can say is that an agency is in business to make money – as, presumably, are copywriters. Nothing much matters to an agency chief except his profitability. Creativity, plaudits and awards are all secondary to the row of figures at the bottom of his performance sheets.

Anybody who tries to make it in advertising with anything other than a philosophy that parallels or reflects this one had better be very, very good. Otherwise, they will shortly be very, very fired.

Rule 2 *Advertising is a business like any other. Results are what matter – profit the motive.*

3 The ad

In some far off, enthusiastic, energetic and ambitious days, I worked for an agency which, by common consent, was certainly among the three best creative outfits in the country – and thinking back, I am probably being charitable to the other two. Why they ever employed me must remain one of the great mysteries of the ages.

This agency had three writers, presided over by a lapsed genius who owned the most biting tongue I've ever been on the wrong side of. I remember rushing into his office one day with a piece of copy which was, in retrospect, far too bombastic for words.

'Will you pass this?' I asked earnestly.

He read the piece quickly and replied: 'Cocker, I think someone already has.'

What distinguished these three writers from the great majority of the legion of copywriters, whose work I have considered since, was the fact that they could write. While each had his or her own particular style and special strengths, they could all turn their hands to anything. Technical ads, consumer ads, fashion ads, soft-sell ads, funny ads, deadpan ads – they could all do the lot and make a good job of it.

They could take a brief consisting of a handful of

nothing and turn it into a thing of advertising beauty, i.e. an ad that pretty well forced you to read it and left you convinced when you had.

The preceding paragraphs have been written not for the purpose of inducing lachrymose nostalgia in me, but rather to graphically illustrate that copywriters should be infinitely adaptable and that formula should never enter their scheme of things.

Ask any marketing-orientated executive (there's some of the jargonized formula) what the constituent parts of an advertisement should be and he will quote the textbook along the following lines.

1   *Headline featuring the main product benefit.*
2   *Opening paragraph enlarging on this benefit.*
3   *Facts to support the benefit claim.*
4   *Warning to reader of what he will miss if he doesn't buy the product.*
5   *Call to action.*

The above formula has, ostensibly, everything to be said in its favour. Except that it very seldom works. Certainly, mediocre advertising can be done by the book and frequently is. But advertising with any kind of life or spark to it results, more often than not, from someone who knows exactly what the book says, but has the nous to know when to fling the book out of the window.

Allow me to give you a very minor example of what I'm talking about. Inoffensive copywriters are often driven into a frenzy by having copy bounced back to them for revision because they've had the temerity to start a sentence with 'and'. They then rush home twitching, speak sharply to their wives, aim random blows at their kids and take to knocking back great bumpers of sherry instead of their usual evening cocoa.

It figures.

This is all because some client or other was, as a child,

rapped over the knuckles and stood in a corner for ignoring the basic principles of grammar. The knuckle-rapping was no doubt deserved; but all it has left him with is an incredible conviction that anyone who kicks off a sentence with 'and' is on a par with the sort of dastard who smokes a cigar with the band on. Which, as you and I know perfectly well, is ridiculous and the mark of literary adolescence.

Thus, on a similar and just as laughable premise, some patently workable ads are kicked out on the grounds that they do not follow the formula, ingredient by strangling ingredient. It's sad, but it happens.

Let me give you another analogy, possibly one closer to your heart. I could (and will if the money is right) write a brisk treatise entitled *'How to seduce a girl in three easy lessons and five minutes flat'*. You would read it. You would be impressed by the sheer logic of it. You would, given the right happy circumstances, apply its precepts. But, if you lack the proper technique, the proper finesse and the proper physiological equipment, you will doubtless end up as unsuccessful and frustrated as the next man.

But things are worse than you may imagine. A fairly large and, for some inexplicable reason, well-respected London agency handles a certain national account which may genuinely be described as more than substantial. (I will forbear from naming the account because I work for it from time to time and I know which side the butter goes on.) Now, this agency produces the client's major advertising campaigns, while a host of provincial firms originates material for local consumption – but under the strict auspices of the London crew.

With conspicuous effrontery, the big agency publishes a 'guidelines document' for dissemination among its carrot-crunching, out of town colleagues. This monstrous document not only sets rules for designing said ads – which is bad enough – but also goes on to instruct the copywriters in the various agencies to employ certain key-words, from a given list, in their headlines and body copy. It's both the height of insolence and just about as inhibiting to the creative mind as you can get.

Is there any wonder that the respective writers (including me) are less than enthusiastic about the work? Can there be any doubt that they put only half their minds to the job?

The moral is clear. Advertising which lives by the book mustn't be at all surprised if it dies by the book. Anybody who knows no other way to judge ads than by a set of rules should look deeply into his soul and consider whether a computer couldn't do his job better.

Rule 3   *Read the book by all means, but don't believe everything you read.*

Having laid a few ghosts, let us take a serious look at what constitutes a good ad.

Whatever the aesthetes may say, and they do tend to say a great deal about nothing, the only way to determine whether an ad is a good one or a bad one is by the way it helps to shift product. In other words, an ad that doesn't create a buying response or, at least, produce a desire to want to know more, is not an ad. Any other considerations for the evaluation of advertising are secondary. Having said that, there are three different kinds of advertisement. 1 The ad that informs the reader of the availability of a product and urges further action. 2 The ad that sells 'off the page' via a coupon – which the likes of Scotcade do remarkably well. 3 The so-called prestige ad, in which a manufacturer or service fills space with self-congratulatory statements purely as a PR exercise. There are also things called blackmail ads. These appear in local peripheral publications like sports programmes, association magazines, and such; and the poor old client is well-nigh forced into appearing in them on account of his refusal would be deemed mealy-mouthed and discourteous.

Ad type number one can be broken down into a myriad of sub-orders. For the sake of brevity, however, and so as not to send you comatose with wadges of detail, we'll examine the two main kinds: the launch ad and the follow-up ad.

In preparing a campaign for any given product, we must first determine the market. Common sense will automatically play a big part here – like, for instance, there's little future trying to promote electric drills in a magazine called *True Life Romances* where the readership might be unmarried girls and women aged between fourteen and thirty. Most of the time, however, products tend not to be so clearly market-defined. Take our Hair Today product. Knowing that this stuff will virtually grow fuzz on billiard balls, it follows that the type of people we want to reach are a complete cross-section of any given population. Their only qualification is that they have to be either completely bald, going bald, or are worried about having baldness thrust upon them.

For all I know, there is a publication called *Bald Monthly* which caters for, commiserates with and offers remedies to cure baldness. If there is, we're laughing. We simply take as much space in that mag as the budget will allow, arrange some sympathetic editorial features – with authenticated tests, and before-and-after pics – and then sit back to wait for the gravy-boat to come steaming in. In reality, we'll have to appear in every kind of media possible to catch the eyes and the interest of the broad spectrum of people we're looking for.

Do we therefore produce just one ad for the lot? In fact, there's no good reason why we shouldn't. A well-prepared, carefully worded launch ad for a product which cures baldness overnight will be as much at home in *The Financial Times* as the *Sun*. We may, of course, be tempted to include a topless blonde in any illustration for the latter paper, but that would only be owing to the fact that the copywriter wants to be in on the photographic session.

So how do we frame the initial thought? Well, the first thing we'll do is work through all the puns of and about hair, hare and heir and, if we have any sense, confine them to the waste-bucket. Then, since our product is so effective and such a blessing to the non-hirsute, we'll say it like it is. That with Hair Today you can have a full head of hair within hours, rather than days – and it will be your own, natural hair.

Simple.

The follow-up ad, or ads, will contain essentially the same message and will reinforce previous claims. We might also incorporate testimonials from satisfied users, especially if they are notable people, to go some way to proving that what we say is genuine.

As part and parcel of the campaign, and running side by side with the launch ad, will be an ad or two aimed at the trade, i.e. chemists, hairdressers, etc. We won't, of course, be approaching hair clinics and such, since they will be too busy taking out high-court injunctions, or finding ways to make a takeover bid.

Now, whether our campaign is selling straight off the page by means of coupons, or we're directing potential buyers to established outlets is largely academic to us. Our marketing boys and girls will have advised the manufacturer in this important respect, and he will either have set up his own direct mail organization, or the marketing people will have worked out ways of 'selling-in' to chemists and hairdressers via reps on the road, mailing, trade advertising, or all three. The creative team will certainly be involved in the preparation of the material for this part of the sales promotion. But, as I say, we don't mind too much which way it's done, because the message will be identical in all instances: only a mug would stay bald when he can have the benefit of hair today.

Which is all very nice and all extremely easy. What happens when we are asked to promote a product that has no obvious benefits over and above it being well manufactured, averagely priced, readily available? Further, what if this product is no better and no worse than half-a-dozen similar products? The answer to both questions is this. We have to work harder and use our imaginations more fully.

Some years back, I worked on an account that manufactured excavators, or mechanical diggers. The products were, without dispute, among the best that money could buy. But so were three similar products made by other digger builders.

How to crack it? How to promote sales of our excavator to the detriment of the others? Indeed, how to help produce the sales to match the fairyland forecasts of an optimistic sales director?

The steps to getting there are these. First, discover everything you can about your excavator and the opposition's excavators. Then compare them. Our aim is to obtain a unique selling proposition (USP).

1 *Mechanically, does our product (X) have anything that (Z) doesn't? Does it work faster? More accurately? What are its limitations as far as digging and shovelling are concerned?*

2 *In terms of engineering, is X better? Are there fewer moving parts, or more moving parts? Does it need less servicing, less maintenance? Does that mean less downtime?*

3 *Price? How does it compare with Z?*

4 *Back-up? Does the manufacturer provide service centres, or mobile servicing units?*

5 *Availability? If I wanted an X right now, could I buy one immediately? What about hiring and leasing? What about financial assistance – does the manufacturer have arrangements with a finance company?*

If, after all this, you discover that your product has no real unique sales point, you now have to try to present it in a unique way – a way that will grab attention, make a sales offer, and be totally different from the opposition's method of presentation.

For what it's worth, this was exactly the impasse we

arrived at with the above-mentioned excavator manufacturer, hereinafter known as Hy-Mac. But, we cracked the
problem, and we cracked it simply, interestingly, and with
lots of emotive demonstration.

Our campaign was to appear in publications that were
read specifically by civil engineers, building contractors and
plant-hire companies. In essence, the opening ad showed an
illustration of a Hy-Mac in action. The excavator was
surrounded by great mounds of earth, its hydraulically-
operated arm was elbow deep in a massive hole, while the
bulk of the machine stood erect, level and safe on the brink. A
stick of copy covered the main benefits of Hy-Mac operation,
buying and hiring availability, and back-up services.

The headline was one of the most concise and pointed I'd
ever written. It simply said:

YOU NEED A HY-MAC

LIKE YOU NEED

A HOLE IN THE GROUND

It won no awards, it even failed to get a mention in *Campaign*.
What it did do, however, was go a long way to convincing a
lot of people that they should have a Hy-Mac on their team.
Sales rose comfortably, the client was delighted, and I was
awarded a large Scotch by the copy chief. (Hy-Mac
eventually went bust. Since I wasn't working on the account
at the time, some other undeserving soul can be saddled with
the credit for its demise.)

In your copywriting life, you will find some products that
have nothing to recommend them whatsoever. They may be
functional – yes, but their whole aspect leaves you cold and
unemotional. They are, in a word, uninspiring. I've met
dozens of them, from patent lids for sealing homemade jam
to what was reputedly the bitterest substance in the world
and which could be added to methylated spirits for the

purpose of preventing certain people drinking it. In my view, the duller and more uninteresting a product is, the brighter and more enthusiastic should be the advertising for it. Being underwhelmed by the nature of a product is no excuse for second-rate work. Jam lids keep many people gainfully employed – so they deserve to be promoted with the same gusto as you would promote a Rolls or an Alfa. The creative input on things like this, then, should be in inverse proportion to their attractiveness.

Take Bryant and May bookmatches. They are tiny, insignificant items, the sole purpose of which is to light once per match, then be discarded forever. You may, or may not, also be aware that said bookmatches are designed to carry advertising messages on their covers. Well, so is just about every other bookmatch product and, as such, is pretty boring and beneath dignity, you may think.

Not a bit of it. Bryant and May employ hundreds, if not thousands of people. Their matches, therefore, need to be sold in volume, and sold to people who also run businesses and who need inexpensive ways of telling the world about their services and goods.

When presented with the initial problem, I got my eyes down with a visualizer and we came up with this. A large picture of the bookmatch cover, complete with fictitious sales message. Resting hugely beside the cover was a spent match. A stick of copy spoke of the economics of advertising on Bryant and May's product, and told how to lay hands on quantities of it. The headline simply ran:

DEATH OF A SALESMAN!

All right, the connotation of snuffing it in relation to a sales message might be seen by many as rather negative, but for capturing attention this ad was a winner all the way.

What of negative advertising – really negative advertising? The 'buy this watch and you'll never want to buy another' types? I hold, and firmly too, that so long as our real message – the point that this watch is so reliable and robust that it will last until eternity – is immediately apparent to even the dimmest of our audience, then negative work is every bit as good as positive work.

Some negative work doesn't work. Like the ad of a dozen years ago which said: 'If the country is going down the drain, it's not your fault . . . it's the fellow standing next to you'. Was that as clear as it might have been? Probably not. I would lay good money that there were plenty of self-satisfied gentry around at the time who read this statement not as a piece of irony, but as a completely straightforward expression of the truth.

You may be wondering how we coped with the afore-mentioned bitterest substance in the world. I'll tell you.

It's called, not unreasonably, Bitrex; and the company which manufactures it saw a market in selling to the makers of branded household cleaners, polishes and the like – products which are not inherently dangerous, but when ingested by youngsters can quite often prove fatal. Now it apparently takes just one tiny drop of Bitrex on the tongue of the average kid to send him running pucker-mouthed and watery-eyed in all directions. Therefore, its minute addition in solution to bleaches, liquid polishes, and domestic chemicals generally would help reduce nasty accidents.

From this, you can see that a little digging and delving transforms an apparently indifferent substance into a property deserving of fuller attention. In seducing the manufacturers of household cleaners into purchasing Bitrex, we made ads with headlines which told them:

LAST YEAR, 5000 CHILDREN WERE ADMITTED TO HOSPITAL WITH A DRINK PROBLEM

(Picture: child with upturned bleach bottle to his lips.)

And:

UNFORTUNATELY, HE WASN'T
OLD ENOUGH TO READ
THE LABEL
(Picture: open cupboard door. Kid prone on floor. Bleach
bottle in foreground up-ended.)

Note the emotive, social-conscience issues raised by these
lines. The message is: stop killing kids; and here's the
product to help you do just that.

Let's move on to ad type two – off-the-page advertising. This
shouldn't be confused with coupon-response advertising (of
which, more later). Off-the-page sells the products as seen in
the ad, for the stated sum, from the address details given. Take
a good, long look at these in the Sunday supplements and you'll
see a strategy sticking out. The strategy goes along these lines:
(a) product picture, (b) bold price figures, (c) punning
headline of and about both the product and the cost: 'Old-
fashioned oil lamps at old fashioned prices', (d) the nature of
the offer – half normal shop price, or cancelled export order
therefore dirt cheap, for instance, (e) turgid and precise
product detail: dimensions, capacities, weight, materials,
colours, (f) how to order details.

Like I say, it's a strategy; and a strategy that has been put
together over many years of trial and error. What's more it
works. Ninety-nine-point-nine per cent of these ads sell, and
sell in a very big way. Some of the best off-the-page work is
done under the auspices of book clubs. It's well thought out,
nicely presented and, above all, in the majority of cases
contains an offer that only a dyslexic could refuse. I suspect
that a great number of book club members have never
opened a volume since they left school, but the prospect of
picking up half-a-dozen books for a pound the lot, negates
their non-erudite proclivities at a stroke.

So much for that. We now come to prestige advertising.

I am generally and generously in favour of prestige advertising (or corporate campaigns as they are more fashionably called) on three counts: commercial, creative and empirical.

Commercial because, let's face it, the fifteen per cent agency commission on every ad placed is fifteen per cent in any language; and campaigns of this nature, if undertaken seriously, need a sizeable and concentrated slice of money spent on them. Creative because they usually provide a well-above-average opportunity for do-as-you-please, distinctive work. Empirical because experience of the nebulous business of advertising tends to show that if handled reasonably, such campaigns may even produce good financial results. But there is one essential difficulty with prestige ads – bearing in mind that they are selling a company as a whole and in the broadest terms, rather than items to be bought. By their very nature they are self-indulgent; they are a case by and large, of preaching not simply to the unconverted but to the totally indifferent.

Take any segment of the populace and you will find that a fair proportion is quintessentially interested in smoking cigarettes, drinking beer, eating sweets, becoming taller, driving cars, wearing brassieres, getting thinner, becoming more beautiful, making money, or doing any of the one thousand and one highly desirable things that ads are made of. But of the same segment, practically nobody has any inherent interest in what a large corporation has to say about itself. It follows, then, that if corporate campaigns are to stand any chance of doing the job they're paid for, they must be striking, original and interesting in their approach. A good deal more so, as it happens, than a campaign for coughdrops, calculators, or cornflakes. In my experience, let it be said, striking, original and interesting are not such adjectives as one can normally apply to them without a stiff tongue in the cheek. Again, in my experience, they are more likely to be pompous, long-winded and dull. With perhaps just a touch tortuous and the oldest of old hat.

We've seen the analogies of tiny acorns growing into massive oaks; we've seen every possible permutation of the door-key and the 'openings' it offers; and we've seen Monopoly boards and chess boards.

Fortunately, we are once in a while allowed the offerings of the like of Shell, Dunlop, BP and others of that standing; some of which is corporate advertising at its very best. But just because the likes of the above lash out millions on their prestige campaigns, it doesn't follow that you can't produce ideas that are as good, if not better, for the engineering company down the road with only a few quid to spend. After all, even the best of ads begin with a blank sheet of paper, just the same as yours will.

*   *   *

One more point, I implore you never to include (if you can even get it past their advertising manager) a picture of a bosomy lady simply for the sake of it, or simply because you can't think of anything else. Bosomy ladies, unless they are selling brassieres, novelty T-shirts, or bust-developers, will do absolutely nothing for your client. True, the decolletage will do wonders for your male readers' respective adrenalins – but will it make them read the bones of your ad, or help them remember the name of the company? I take leave to doubt it.

I'll put it another way. The let's-show-a-nude school of advertising assumes (rightly) that buyers don't have all that much objection to seeing a little nature in the raw. But when they go on to assume (wrongly) that an expanse of navel, bottom, or thigh is likely to put their point over for them, they are definitely barking up the wrong pin-up. What I always say is that if you can't write advertising on a given subject without majoring on something completely irrelevant to it, then it's high time you considered whether it might not be wiser to write something else – like fiction.

A lot of other people say the same. So now you know why not every corporate campaign (or any other kind of campaign come to that) features a nude.

Rule 4 *You are by profession, or soon will be, a cliché recycler. But some clichés are worn so thin, they won't stand further peddling.*

Summary

1 The three main ad types are:
   (a) *Consumer/industrial/technical.* An announcement about the product, or service, and where it may be obtained.
   (b) *Off-the-page.* A direct-selling device that solicits money in exchange for goods.
   (c) *Prestige.* A proclamation about a company, rather than about a product. Also known as corporate advertising.
2 Formula is for chemists. As with any other kind of commercial creativity (songwriting, illustrating, photography) the preparation of advertising is an essentially hit-and-miss business. And there's nothing to be ashamed of in that.
3 Before putting pen to paper, dig deeply into the facts, figures and benefits of the product. Insist on examining it first-hand, or demand a demonstration of its capabilities. Try to make yourself as familiar with the product as the fellow who produces it.
4 Unearth the USP. Decide how it makes your product different from any other of its kind. Then allow your mind to wander all around the proposition, with the purpose of putting yourself into the shoes of the type of person who might spend money to own it.

5   Every product, no matter how dull and uninteresting it may be to you, will be of singular interest to someone. Once you discover who, you'll know why. And once you find out why, *you'll know how.*

Not that I'm advocating that ads should lie or deliberately mislead (not while the Trades Description Act is still in force, anyway). But there is, to my mind such a thing as advertising licence. By emphasis, and by *omission of detail* that would only be relevant to the reader if he actually possessed the product (like how to switch it on, open the lid, or assemble it), one can add a touch of showmanship that lifts the piece out of the prosaic.

A great proportion of advertising may have its facts straight and its figures adding up, yet it is, it must be said, something that only its parent could love. Which, believe me, is often the case.

Rule 6   *Spending hard-won appropriations of money simply to bore people is one of the less intelligent pastimes of this life.*

Striking next. And here, much advertising is inclined to break its neck in a frantic search for reader-stopping gimmicks. I'll grant that many ads could justifiably be called striking; but what they often strike me as is plain foolish. Spending cash to project yourself as a bunch of clowns really is a waste.

I have in front of me now a whole depressing sheaf of assorted ads which have gone overboard in their efforts to attract my attention. Since I am in a charitable mood, I will refrain from mentioning and naming them. The kind of ads I'm talking about suffer, among other things, from the cardinal sin of irrelevance. They set out to sell, say, cushion flooring; but because a floor is a floor is a floor and isn't the most photogenic of items, they decide to illustrate instead an executive jet aircraft. They then tie themselves in knots trying to explain that people who use their flooring end up by flying in executive jets because of the savings they make.

That sort of foolishness.

The point is that executive jets may be very noble in themselves, but have little to do with cushion flooring.

As an aside, here, you may well chime in with the thought that nobody has the right to knock an ad unless they (a) have a precise idea of the marketing strategy behind it and, less importantly perhaps, (b) know whether and how it was mucked about by all and sundry between typewriter and publication.

Very true.

All advertising is, or should be, created in the context of a marketing strategy, and I'll agree there is often a good deal more to an ad than meets the eye. Not so many years ago, a leading insurance company ran a full-page, full-colour campaign in a number of Sunday supplements and similar media, the space in which cannot be bought for peanuts. It was addressed, ostensibly, to the man in the street. However, it achieved the lowest reading-and-noting figures in one of those tedious copy-research exercises in which I have so very little faith. To take notice of that, though, would have been to miss the many-splendoured marketing thing. Because this campaign, although it talked to the general public, was not, in fact, aimed at the general public. It was a sprat to catch a mackerel, and its intended purpose was to generate a rapid increase in the number of agents for the company. The national consumer advertising was, in effect, trade advertising; and in these terms it was a resounding success.

So you really never know. But *most* ads are trying to do what they appear to be trying to do; and the average reader of them is in precisely the same position as I am – he neither knows, nor particularly cares what the strategy or planning behind them is. He, and we, take them at their face value and form an opinion on that.

No, I am right behind an ad that gets an unfair share of attention – but it will never, ever do so if it employs irrelevant comparisons.

Anyway, comparisons are odious.

* * *

Did you know that even today in advertising circles, many arguments still rage about the merits of 'long' body copy over 'short' body copy? One would have thought that after all these years, the thing would have long been resolved. Maybe I should resolve it right now. Long copy, I am given to understand, is anything over fifty words, short is anything under.

Why do they quibble? Why do they rail? Well, some say that nobody reads copy anyway. Others say that copy is a mandatory part of every ad.

They are both wrong on both counts. People do, and it isn't. And if you think I'm being contradictory, you're right –but also wrong.

There exists a line of opinion which maintains that no ad is complete without a stick of body copy in it. A stick of body copy, therefore, is what their ads invariably get – never mind whether they have anything worth saying or not.

On the other hand, there are those who set their faces sternly against copy – long or short – again irrespective of whether the story they have to tell demands copy (long or short).

Both parties, again, are equally in error.

Copy for copy's sake, without life, without interest, and without story is less than useless. If you have nothing of any interest to say to the reader, either don't say it, or at least say it in such a manner that the style itself will disguise the basic lack of real content. Conversely, no copy for no copy's sake, might just leave your audience, your potential customers, hopping from foot to foot with a dozen questions on their lips; and there's nothing to provide the answers. Even worse, the general public being what it is, simple, but very shrewd and certainly not daft, will walk away from the ad with but two thoughts. 1. That the whole thing is some kind of con, and if they do make the effort to contact the advertiser an unwholesome sack of rats will be let loose upon them. 2. That maybe they'll get around to finding out more when they have the time. Like next week, perhaps.

Not unexpectedly, I am a great believer in copy. Enough copy, that is, to satisfy anyone who wants to know more. I also believe that it can be done without when the occasion demands.

Even so, those no-copy ads should contain more than no copy. Don't rush off with the idea that all you have to do in these instances is make a simple headline statement, which includes the name of the advertiser, drop in his logo, and the job's done. I find these ads both curious and depressing. And, as I'm sure you know, there are enough of them about to make me so.

Anyone's name, it's true, is precious to him. Everyone loves the sound of his own monicker. One might go so far as to say that there is nothing the average person would rather hear. But your name, I must confess, wouldn't particularly excite me – just as mine, presumably, doesn't excite you. So what is the percentage in running an ad that just says who the advertiser is, or where he lives; or, at best, what he does for a living? Remarkably little, if you ask me.

Methinks anyone who goes in for this kind of advertising presumes too much. Furthermore, if an ad says nothing and shows nothing, it is tacitly admitting that it has nothing worth saying or worth showing.

They would gain more benefit from putting their money on a three-legged outsider.

So as for believing that nobody reads copy – twaddle! Any human being, when he or she is *in the market* for a new car or a new set of golf clubs, will read everything on new cars and golf clubs that happens to come their respective ways. And I do mean everything: the facts, the figures, the prices, the places – the lot.

You do. I do. Isn't that right? But, you'll also agree, only provided that:

1   *They have been induced to do so via the headline, the illustration, or both.*

2   *The copy is sufficiently well written to make it worth reading.*
3   *The copy tells them something, or reminds them of something worth knowing.*

Alas, these three criteria are so seldom fulfilled that, when they are, one's heart leaps as Wordsworth's must have done when he clapped his eyes on all those daffs. (For examples of recent ads that live up to these standards, see pages 109 to 125.) The cold, lifeless porridge served up in so many ads – especially industrial ads – is so moribund that one wonders why the people concerned went to the expense of incurring typesetting costs. Some are the equivalent of business letters which begin: 'We are in receipt of your esteemed favour of the thirtieth ultimo and beg leave to thank you for same'. And there are plenty of those still floating around – probably authored by the people responsible for the kind of copy I'm carping about.

In my more despondent moments, it sometimes seems to me that the great bulk of industrial advertising (and some consumer material, too) is conceived by a committee whose basic literary diet is civil service minutes.

They are a committee because the handiwork bears the stigma of too many cooks, and of sundry people insisting on chucking in their two-penn'orth. They are a committee on account of they suppose that the whole world is either fully familiar with their product, or is waiting with baited breath to learn of it. And they are literary civil servants because the words they use to sell with are so dead as to make the dodo seem like an emergent chick.

They use words like 'expertise', which is a red rag to me. They employ incongruous clauses like 'skilled craftsmen'. And they clog up the lexicographic works with frightful-nesses like 'produced under strictly controlled conditions for exacting construction by the most modern methods'.

How much easier to say: *We really know our business – and we can prove it.* Or: *We think you'll be impressed with our workmanship.*

With reinforcement of the statement by giving a few examples of how the product is put together. Or: *Every component is thoroughly tested before it is built into the product.* Then drive home the claim with details of how those tests are carried out.

The alternatives, you may concur, are so much easier to assimilate, understand and believe. And that, after all, is the object of the exercise. Good copy consists of ordinary, everyday words woven into ordinary, everyday sentences. Nothing more.

You may not yet have had the dispassionate and cynical pleasure of watching one of those 'committee' advertisers leafing through a publication in which one of his ads appears. He has eyes for nothing else. He turns page after impatient page until his baby turns up; then he pounces upon it like a swooping owl and studies it with the intensity of Sherlock Holmes putting a glass to a flake of tobacco-ash on a suspect's lapel.

Advertisers are, of course, perfectly right to be deeply interested in their own efforts. But the mistake many make is to assume that their audience is equally interested. Let's say it again. If an ad doesn't communicate in simple terms and simple language, it will be by-passed pretty rapidly by those less interested in the niceties of syntax than you are or I am.

Rule 7 *If it doesn't communicate, it won't sell. And if it doesn't sell, it isn't advertising.*

You'll have noticed that I make quite a lot of reference to industrial-type advertising in these pages. The explanation is that we (and I'm now talking specifically to those on the point of entering the business) shouldn't kid ourselves in any way that when we eventually breeze into an agency we'll be working on plum consumer accounts as a matter of course. We won't.

Of the eight hundred and fifty-odd agencies in the UK, only a fraction have accounts with appropriations which might decently be called blue-chip. Meaning £3,000,000 to spend, or more. In fact, the large proportion cannot boast a total agency billing (the sum spent by all of their clients combined) of very much more than that amount.

So if you're expecting to be working on the likes of, say, British Airways, Cadbury-Schweppes, Rowntree Mackintosh and British Rail, you certainly do have great expectations. Much more likely, you'll be knocking out stuff for lower echelon advertisers who have less than massive budgets. Many of these will be industrial firms selling everything from nuts and bolts to hydraulic presses; and commercial outfits marketing unit trusts and self-managed pension funds. Lumped together, we could more properly call them semi-technical accounts. They are the cornerstone of UK advertising, generating accumulatively an enormous sum in advertising revenue; but taken by themselves in small doses, they're unlikely even to make page-ten news in *Campaign*.

Notwithstanding that, your efforts on their behalf will be sterling. They'd better be – your job will depend on it.

* * *

A lot of industrial ads (and a lot of non-industrial ads, come to that) start off in life with a nasty initial drawback. They have, as we've already discussed, nothing particular to say about the products they are promoting. At the same time, it comes to pass in every copywriter's life that he or she tires of writing about brick-making machines, forklift trucks, lubricants, insulants, solvents and eccentric gears. Not only tired, but sick with it. This is especially the case when a writer has worked constantly on a given account over a number of years and has gone irretrievably stale. Not that it should ever be admitted, of course; a real professional always appears to be coming up with the goods no matter how chocker he feels.

There are times, though, when staleness is purely in the

jaundiced eye of the beholder. For instance, a freelance of my acquaintance worked for an agency on a double-glazing account for a period of some four years. We'll call them agency A. Now it happened that, for whatever reason, the client decided his advertising needed some fresh thinking. Thus, he invited a number of other agencies to get their acts together and put up proposals in the shape of full-blown campaigns. Quite naturally, agency A became uneasy at the prospect of that fat fee departing to another outfit. So, in their wisdom, they decided that for this exercise they would give their loyal, but purportedly jaded freelance a rest and, in the event, called in a fresher mind to do the work. Meantime, however, the said exhausted freelance was approached by agency B to put some ideas on paper for their presentation. This he could ethically do since he was no longer employed by A.

There are no prizes for guessing that B won the account; with chagrin aplenty on the A team.

Any old how, while both the lack of unique selling proposition in the product and staleness on the part of the writer are sad, they are understandable. After all, no matter how long you may have been at it, what exactly is the sellable difference between one brand of British-standard steel rod and another?

Echo answers – what?

In such circumstances, given this 'we've-got-space-to-fill-but-nothing-to-say' situation, many a desperate wordsmith leaps gratefully on the back of that reliable old nag called service.

Service ads, in effect, say: *We're a great bunch of lads.* They then go on to proclaim: *What's more, by crikey, when you tell us to jump, we jump – and we stay up there until instructed to come down.*

I have nothing at all against service and civility being used as a peg on which to hang an ad, or even an entire campaign for that matter. Indeed, I have been grateful for these essentially amorphous terms on many an occasion. Yet they

4   More about the ad

The primary task of advertising, it has been mooted, is to present a beautiful, exact and striking description of the nature and quality of the goods advertised.

Let us, for the good of our souls, spend a moment or two considering this dictum in relation to advertising generally.

Beauty, particularly with regard to advertising the many hard-nosed technical products which one has flung upon one's desk from time to time, doesn't necessarily mean chi-chi, or fancy, or indirect. It is possible to spend a few pounds and have a photographer take a beautiful shot of, say, a phosphor-bronze shell-bearing. Very possible. In these terms, beauty is a virtue of which most technical/industrial advertising is singularly bereft.

We now come to the word exact. The one thing you can't accuse much of today's advertising of being is inexact. On the contrary, much tends to be too exact for its own good – in two ways. First, by forcing into the space more fact than it will sensibly accommodate, thereby serving up ads which may be full of vitamins, but which are totally indigestible. Second, by insisting on such precision of detail that they end up by being more like data sheets than advertisements.

Rule 5   *In baiting a mousetrap with cheese – always leave room for the mouse.*

35

should in no way whatsoever be made the scapegoats for such visual and verbal absurdities as one comes across betimes. The worst of recent months having illustrations of men in white overalls literally bending over backwards; of a city gent astride a rocking-horse telling us that nobody is on their high horse at so-and-so's; and of a half-naked woman making the point that since she gets serviced regularly at a certain garage, you should do likewise.

There is a word for material like this. Come to think of it, there are several words. Farther than that, I am not prepared to go.

*   *   *

And now for the ubiquitous coupon; its function; its use as an ad-testing gauge via the response it elicits; and the potential terrors of a nil response.

Without wishing to insult your intelligence, a coupon is merely a device for encouraging punters to find out more about your products or services. This can be achieved with the offer of free literature, or the attendance of a company consultant in their own homes. The consultant is, of course, a salesman who will do everything in his power to 'convert' the coupon response into a sale. There are variations on the theme of what a coupon offers, but these are the main considerations. A coupon can also provide the client with a very worthwhile catalogue of potential customers which he can readily turn into a mailing-list, or house-call list, for future operations.

The astute will no doubt already have realized that the inclusion of a coupon in an ad could spell disaster for the agency if a client is overly optimistic – if he expects better results than he actually gets. Worse still is the opprobrium when a client has been sold a bill-of-goods by a too enthusiastic account executive, with talk of percentage response that's beyond his wildest dreams.

Forecasting the response one might get from a coupon is a divertisement comparable to that of accurately predicting the time and date of the end of the world. It can't be done with much precision. Ordinarily, though, you can keep your fingers crossed for a coupon return in the neighbourhood of two and a half per cent if your ad is well made and given that you've hit the right media for the market. On a good day, a red-letter day, you might make eight per cent. It doesn't happen often.

Money-off coupons, incidentally, are a different kettle of fish. I've seen redemptions on these going through thirty per cent. But in this instance, you're waving what amounts to filthy lucre under people's noses. And that they like.

Taking it in the round, coupons are a fine idea if nobody demands too much from them – a bad idea if they do.

Once upon a time, someone was dredging into the farther reaches of his invention in an attempt to come up with a coupon ad with a difference. Suddenly, an idea hit him with the impact of a sockful of wet sand. Why not make an ad that was all coupon?

One of the first ads of this type, as far as I am able to determine, was for Alfa Romeo. It was conceived by the man who originally trained me. (He taught me everything I know. What a pity he didn't teach me everything he knew.)

Disdaining, not without a modicum of courage, to illustrate any of Alfa's very superior motor cars, the ad simply showed a coupon, inside which sat a headline saying: '*This is a smooth, imperious, powerful, 105 m.p.g. coupon – with a beautiful little five-speed gearbox.*' There was a touch of copy to it, but very little; and basically the whole thing was a headline-cum-coupon ad.

This was fine; and so were some of its successors, not to mention any of its possible predecessors. Nowadays, however, it is difficult to open any given newspaper or magazine and not find some ad or other which hinges more or less entirely on a coupon. And I confess to being exasperated by all of it.

Enough is enough – and is rapidly becoming too much. Any writer, therefore, who is tempted to do something nice and tricksy with a coupon would do well to remember that practically everything tricksy has already been done with a coupon. Not only done, but overdone; and by just everyone. Including me.

'Don't cut the coupon – rip out the page' was one of my better efforts.

Something else; and maybe some latter-day Freud could come up with an answer. I continue to be intrigued by the fact that when returning a coupon, most people will insist on cutting studiously along the dotted line. Why?

Summary

1   Putting too much detail into an ad can be most thoroughly destructive. I am not, decidedly not, talking about those retail-type pieces which cram the page with a variety of product-pictures, descriptions and prices. They are astoundingly good workers – for the reason that they furnish just enough detail about each item to whet the appetite. The delinquents are those which go on and on like a Victorian monograph, to exhaust both the subject and the reader.

2   Acting the giddy goat in print, by employing idiotic metaphors of people 'turning somersaults to please', is an insult to the reader's intelligence. Worse, it projects the advertiser as a bumpkin and makes him a laughing stock, rather than an affable, hard-working vassal who will go out of his way to give the customer what he wants – which is what its author presumably intended.

3   I have never seen the point of using patently irrelevant comparisons. Employing one product (usually a superior one, otherwise there would be no reason for the exercise) to promote another product more often than

not results in the reader spending his time – if he spends any – drooling over the better product.

You may be interested to know that until a few years ago, so many copywriters were press-ganging the superlative Rolls Royce product into service in this context that the company broke its characteristic silence and promised, I believe, to start suing the offenders.

And rightly so.

4   There can be no doubt, people do read copy. But one or two businessmen I know, for instance, say they never read ads – more pertinently, perhaps, they say they never read mailing shots. They then go on to suggest that nobody else does, either. This sort of stupidity ranks alongside those who maintain that they are absolutely and totally uninfluenced, in any shape or respect, by advertising.

In one way or another everybody is influenced by advertising – although the exact how, why, when and where is indefinable. And, at some time or another, everybody reads body copy – including that which is contained in mailing shots.

5   A coupon will be responded to only if your major proposition is sufficiently tempting. Unquestionably, there are enough compulsive fillers-in of coupons about to save you, most times, from the disgrace of a zero response. But your client will be looking for 'coupon conversions' – eventual sales – not a co-entry in the *Guinness Book of Records* with someone who has a roomful of said client's colour brochures.

5　Copy philosophy

People starting in this business are wont to tell me that every rule of grammar they ever learned is completely redundant in advertising. They also point out, quite acidly, that decent English is not only disregarded, but also has no place whatsoever in copywriting.

Who am I to argue? But I will anyway. What I suggest we do, to try to show that copy English shouldn't necessarily be synonymous with slovenly English is establish a number of fundamentals.

First　Let's establish between us that grammar is made for man – and not the other way around. Let us also say that language is a living thing which certainly must have rules, but just as certainly shouldn't be hindered by them. Someone once said that changes in language are the result of years of inventive illiteracy. This may very well be true, but I maintain that copy can be inventive without loss of basic scholarship.

Second　Let's determine exactly what we're attempting to do when we write copy. No bones about it, we're doing our best to communicate with a lot of people who genuinely do not want to play our game.

Third　In the so doing, we are forced to make contact via the minimum number of words, in order that the reader will get the message with the minimum effort on his part.

Fourth   Were we to adopt a strict grammatical stance, or a rigid syntactic strategy, we'd lose the reader mid-yawn. Every sentence would read as though it fell from the nib of Thackeray which, however sadly, would be received with a profound ho-hum by the readers of your average daily paper. Such usage would be an abusage of the punter.

Fifth   When you are out gallivanting, meeting people in pubs and similar joyous places, you communicate with them in what is colloquially known as the vernacular. You say it like it acceptably is. You would be wise, therefore, to do exactly the same when you write copy.

When I worked for a Dublin agency, I learned the patois in very short order – because my London-framed idioms were being met with perplexed stares. The same also applied when I was with Scottish and Miami agencies. Which probably goes a long way to explaining why my writing is a hotch-potch of all that's worst in standard Irish/Scots/American/English.

Sixth   When writing ads, you must be all things to all people – just as a good salesman is. You temper your style, adjust your delivery, and manufacture your tone according to the socio-economic status of the audience. Thus, when you talk to the medical profession, you do so in a manner that appeals to their sensibilities and which will hold their attention. Similarly, if you talk to musicians, you've got to make it appear that you have a more than passing acquaintanceship with their business. This sometimes results in the kind of grammar that isn't as accurate as it might be; but the writing can be all the more interesting because of that.

Permit me to put it another way. Copywriters become sick and tired of having material rejected by self-righteous clients claiming (usually correctly) that the stuff is ungrammatical.

'You have,' they often declare, 'split an infinitive. What's worse, you have done so more than once.'

Heaven forfend! Leave this sort of thing uncastigated, and where's it all going to end? Next thing you know, everybody will be starting sentences with 'but' and ending them with prepositions. Or even vice versa. From there, it's only a matter of time before the whole country is overrun by football hooligans. And they, as we all know, would split an infinitive as soon as look at it.

I suggest that there are worse things than splitting infinitives – one of which is splitting hairs. I am also led to suspect that most people would remain completely unmoved in the presence of an asundered infinitive.

The design boys are lucky. Very few clients would dream of physically 'correcting' a visual or an illustration; and that's mostly because very few people have the ability to draw well. But lay a sheet of inventive copy in front of them and out comes the old biro.

I am bound to say that some copy would make the style of ransom notes and letters to Father Christmas seem positively Wildean. But this sort of stuff is not usually produced by professionals.

There is one rule of English, however, which I absolutely insist upon in copy. In all copy. When talking directly of and about the company in question, always stick to the matey first person plural 'we', or the genitive plural 'our', rather than the very impersonal and horribly brusque 'they'. It looks better; it sounds better; and it works better.

I could go on to the seventh, eighth and even twentieth places, and one day no doubt I will. But let's get back to copy.

Given the above criteria, who's the arbiter of good English? Never mind. Just remember what I've said and decide, here and now, that you are a communicator, not an educator.

To move on to more blithesome themes, I ask you to consider the case for humour in advertising. Does it work? Is it mandatory? Is it relevant? And, if so, why and how?

Quite often, when an agency is stuck for a positive idea for an ad or a campaign, and lacks the gall to present the client with something based on an aerial picture of his factory (a singularly pathetic device which, to be fair, is more often than not forced upon the agency by the client), it is likely to turn to humour for its salvation. After all, at a pinch, we can always be funny about anything.

The avenue of escape, however, is certain to be full of pitfalls, since a sense of humour is something that tends to differ sharply from one person to another; and in some unfortunate individuals, to be absent altogether.

It takes, I think it true to say, all sorts; and this to me is sound enough reason for approaching humour in advertising with a good deal of caution.

If you run a straight ad which doesn't prove to be up to scratch, its effect may well be neutral. It probably doesn't do much active harm either. But if you attempt to be funny and fail miserably, then the effect of the advertising may be positively injurious. Faced with something that seems to him veritably plain daft, a reader (or viewer and listener, come to that) may be excused for thinking that the advertiser is a wally. And one doesn't normally choose to do business with wallies.

Nevertheless, the campaigns which move into the public consciousness quickest and stay there longest tend to be the funny ones. Ask anyone which advertising he remembers and I will give you a shade of odds that the Fosters 'Aussie in Britain', the Pils 'film clips' and the Heineken 'refreshes the parts' campaigns will be among the first mentioned.

Ask a similar question on the industrial side, and I shall be very surprised if the names Desoutter and Accles and Pollock don't crop up a darned sight more often than most.

It would seem, then, that there is gold in them there smiles – provided you write and design them in a genuinely funny way. I emphasize genuine because if you are not one hundred per cent convinced that what you are proposing will tickle fancies right and left, you would be better advised to get that picture of the factory organized.

I once wrote a mildly humorous ad (not my only humorous ad, by the way) for the Portuguese airline TAP. It contained a large black and white picture of a Boeing 707 in flight. Below that was a second, smaller picture in full colour; it showed the dinner-tray and typical food served by this airline. The headline said: *'Nobody ever walked out because the food was bad'*.

Well, I said it was mildly humorous; and whether you smiled or not is completely academic. For when I wrote the ad, I missed one very important issue: something like sixty per cent of all air-passengers are terrified of flying. So not only did I take the initial risk of appealing to the sense of fun of only a fraction of my audience (humour being the nebulous thing it is), more than half the audience already found nothing funny about flying anyway.

See what I mean?

Rule 8 *People don't buy from clowns – and that includes clients.*

* * *

Which brings us nicely to the pun. Without doubt, the pun is endemic to the average British copywriter. And the more average he is, the more endemic it is likely to be. It is in his blood; and it is there because he believes it is expected of him.

It ain't – not by me it ain't.

One hardly dares open a magazine these days for fear of being punned to death. The little devils appear in headlines, in body copy, even in tag-lines. (A tag-line is that phrase usually placed beneath the company logo. It sets out to give a concise philosophy of the firm, and a nice warm feeling to the reader. Invariably, though, it's an impediment that says nothing and means less.)

I think you know what I'm getting at, but for fun we'll take a few random and distressing examples of the pun. A recent campaign for a well-known tool manufacturer gave us a hammer pictured in the contrived guise of a boxer. That should have been plenty enough warning to the student of the pun, since one could practically close one's eyes and recite the copy. It had allusions to champions, to ringing the bell and never throwing in the towel, to heavyweights, to punches being packed – and to any of the other one hundred and one pugilistic references.

The torch that this company carries with such egregious distinction (throughout its entire product range, incidentally) burns brightly in the hearts of many another advertiser.

There is a company manufacturing luggage which tells us: 'let's get down to cases,' along with a picture of . . . yes . . . a judge. Another, which for its sins makes zip-fasteners, insists it is in the 'security business,' reinforcing this with an illustration of a uniformed security guard. There's a third making some kind of labelling machine that assures us they have 'a name' for doing just that.

It's a case of piling Pelion upon Ossa if ever there was one. Yet example mounts on tedious example. Manufacturers of domestic cleaning fluids can't seem to get over the happy linguistic fact that their solutions provide solutions to problems. People who offer to cut costs, lend a hand, undertake mammoth jobs and tailor their services show: scissors, hands, elephants and tape-measures respectively.

I'd have thought that, by now, this penchant for maltreating the obvious would have had its execrable day. I would be wrong, of course. As each new generation of eager-Pentelled copywriters comes along, it stumbles upon this rich vein of worked-over puns and fancies it has found Eldorado.

Someone should speak to it – like I am trying to do.

I don't dislike puns – not if they are appropriate, apt and original puns. As an example, let me run a pun-type ad for Peter Stuyvesant cigarettes past you. This ad appears in full colour. It shows the pack with several cigarettes raised out of it; and the pack is superimposed over a night shot of New

York skyscrapers. Length is the impression we are asked to gain – which is definitely the impression we get. The headline runs: *'As long as it's Peter Stuyvesant'*.

A good pun, an appropriate pun and, as far as I know, a by-no-means overdone pun. I applaud it; as I do the other ads in that particular campaign.

Be cautious, then, before you rush off in all directions shouting eureka because of some brilliant idea you've just had. Immerse yourself in the agency guardbook – cuttings of past ads. Chances are you'll find that whiz-bang of a pun you are about to commit yourself to is mouldering away in some yellowing tome.

* * *

We now come to the exclamation mark. Its abuse and misuse.

Until a few years ago, I was as guilty of this folly as the next chap; but a kindly soul pointed out the error of my ways, since when I have been proselytizing with the best of them.

I sometimes feel that if all the typesetting houses were to withdraw the exclamation mark from their spec sheets, half the copywriters in the country would be tongue-tied. The screamer, as I'm sure you know, is meant to indicate a scream. It should not be peppered willy-nilly at the end of a few random sentences as a kind of show of force. Nor, in particular, should it be stationed after puns, mild jokes and throwaway lines to say, in effect, that what went before was designed to be funny.

This last and disturbingly widespread practice is both coy and, if you analyse it, insulting to the reader. The screamer is also misguidedly used to indicate urgency or immediacy. In my opinion it does neither; and its use in this respect does no credit to the writer either.

You often come across this same sort of precipitancy in radio commercials. These end with an emphasis which implies not only a pair of screamers, but underlined italics into the bargain.

I was listening, just the other day, to a local commercial radio station when on came a thirty-second spot for a brand of sunglasses. It ended, after much hollering and shouting, with an exhortation to 'get out and buy your sunglasses – right now!'

The time of this particular broadcast was around 12.30 on a Sunday – an hour when most women are up to their elbows in roast beef and two veg, most men are up to their ears in pints of ale, and most chemists are either closed or, more likely, inhibited by some curious law from selling anything other than Aspro and corn-plasters.

Whether the advertiser expected everyone to drop their Yorkshires, bolt their beers, and to stream out and hammer on the doors of unresponsive chemists' shops, I don't know. It would obviously be foolish to make any kind of issue out of the timing of this commercial. Or, indeed, its exhortation ending. I cite it only as an example of how, via the spoken as well as the written word, the innocent exclamation mark is continuously taking a hammering that it neither deserves nor asks for.

It all stems, I suppose, from those well-meaning books on copywriting without tears which insist, nay demand, that every piece of copy should finish with a bang, a flourish of verbal trumpets and an injunction to buy.

Such works have caused more mischief in the minds of the half-informed than they have ever done good. Because the best of copy nowadays (not the majority, but the best) ends with a whisper rather than a bang; and the writers of it are sensible enough to realise that the injunction to buy does not lie solely in the final punchline, but is inherent in the whole ad from top to bottom.

So to close this mini-tirade about nothing much, my clear advice on the subject is this: when tempted to put down a screamer . . . think twice!! Then think again!!!

Don't, please, take me up wrongly. My brand of wisdom,

for want of a better word, is no more desirable than the brand X of many another copywriter. But over the years, a number of things have tended to irritate, and I think it's about time I scratched the itch. In the so-doing, if you learn something from it – or simply believe you've learned something from it – so much the better.

*   *   *

We shall now discuss the arguments about hard-sell and soft-sell. If you aren't familiar with these terms, I'll put you straight. Hard-sell is said to be that type of advertising which shouts at you, bullies you and hopes to leave you with the impression that you are something of a mug, seeing as how you don't already own whatever it is they're talking so loudly about. Soft-sell by comparison, is alleged to be the sort which creeps up on you on the quiet, makes you nod sagely, and hints in the subtlest possible way that there's a mite more to what they're selling than is obvious at first glance.

There is, I contend, good and bad of both kinds. Were you to demand a definite opinion, I would come down on the side of the soft-sell every time. Here's why.

A lot of advertisers, and thus a lot of their copywriters, are in private life perfectly reasonable human beings. But they seem to be under some compulsion to bawl their heads off in print. Personally, I believe that when you shout about something that manifestly isn't worth shouting about, you only succeed in making yourself look idiotic. On the other hand, just as the soft answer turneth away wrath, so the soft statement frequently turneth on the customer.

In our deadly-earnest, hard-selling, seventy-two point headline, all-singing, all-dancing world, when so many ads are banging the big drum, those which have the courage to do no more than perform a modest melody on a lively sax stand that much more chance of being heard.

Hard-sell, the material that will have no truck with such

irrelevancies as humour, innuendo and subtlety, appeals to a great many advertisers. It appeals, especially, to those people without the imagination to realize that gentle persuasion is not only much more rewarding than brute force, but is also likely to allow one the splendid opportunity to go back and have a second go. Because the hard stuff is brisker and more to the point, they imagine it must necessarily be more effective.

This is a contention that just won't hold water.

If you need a precept, here it is. Resist the temptation to inject a fancied urgency into your headlines by the inclusion of an imperative *now!* If you have something to 'now' about, fair enough; but if you haven't, your headline will almost certainly be stronger without it. The same goes for *look!* and *suddenly!* and similar bring-'em-up-short words. In the right context, they're fine; though if you start saying the equivalent of *suddenly . . . nothing much happened!* don't be surprised if you suddenly get nothing much in the way of response.

Over the years, I have grown weary and dispirited trying, with ninety-eight per cent lack of success, to persuade sundry Philistines that the above principle of advertising is immutable. They mostly continue to ignore me. So since there is no profit in banging your head against a brick wall if all you get out of it is a blinding headache, I will say no more about it.

If you are in any way serious about this copy business, you should from now on spend much of your time reading ads. Try to discover why one ad appeals to you more than another. Is it because of the message it delivers, or the way it delivers the message? Is it on account of the illustration, or the drift of the copy – or both? Which of the main components drew you into the ad in the first place? While you're at it, exercise your mind on various ways of 'improving' the ads you like – either in the headline, the copy, or the illustration. And be not surprised when, a few days later, you come across ads in the same series framed roughly along the lines of those you dreamed up.

When this happens, give yourself a pat on the back. But bear in mind that you haven't originated – just developed. We shall be talking about origination in the following chapter.

Summary

1   As far as copy English is concerned, there is but one thing left to say. In this book we are concerned only with general principles; and if general principles clash with pedantic rules then so much the worse for pedantic rules.

2   Humour and good taste rarely go hand-in-hand. A joke is almost always funny *because* of its doubtful taste. In being humorous, therefore, you run the risk of offending at least some of your audience. But in being downright inane, you run the risk of displeasing all of them. To paraphrase Lord Chesterfield: A man must have a good deal of wit himself to endure a great deal in another.

3   On the subject of puns, I should like to offer a simple – though far from foolproof – method by which to tell whether the pun you propose to use is old and well worn, or new and hardly touched. First, stop to consider how the idea came to you. Did it appear within moments of starting to wrestle with the project? Did it slip into your mind word-perfect, with no call for amendment? If you answer yes to both these questions, then the chances are that your intended pun is old enough to qualify for a telegram from Buckingham Palace.

4   Not long ago, I acquired a private pilot's licence. A bit late in the day, perhaps, but I acquired it nevertheless. Now, flying is a serious business – a very serious business. So when I first set out to find a flying instructor who would show me the ropes (relieving me, at the same time, of several thousand pounds), I chose not the young, brash, fast-talking individual from flying club A, but the

softly-spoken almost self-effacing old-timer from club B. Both were eminently qualified to do the job, yet Mr B inspired me with much greater confidence. That, effectively, is the difference between hard-sell and soft-sell.

And if you are ever privileged enough to fly with Wing-Commander Jock Dalgleish, you'll know exactly what I mean.

6   The headline

It is, I suppose, revealing no deep trade secrets to say that ours is a frenetic and pressurizing kind of business. Advertising doesn't have its high ulcer-rate and its even higher mental exhaustion rate for nothing. We are all of us constantly being fretted and goaded into the pursuit of something new – largely for newness' sake; which is never the best of reasons.

One of the most damning and deflating things anyone can say to a copywriter or designer about an idea he has in mind is: 'It's been done before, you know'. This leaves you with the sort of feeling you might experience when attending a party to which you have been invited in error. But the more I think about it, the more it seems that the 'done before' remark, whether meant as a snide comment or a helpful one, has probably killed off more reasonable ads than it has ever stifled imitative ones.

Let's face it, everything has been done before in one form or other; but most things will stand quite a lot of imaginative re-working. The emphasis, in so far as ideas are concerned, is on re-working; we are not talking about straight repetition.

As an example of that, consider if you will the trite, but still very evident headline: *'You get more for your money with a Damson home computer'*. I would ask you, also, to assume that the body copy accompanying such a line would speak of

63

more bytes, more software, and more this and that for the price. Yes, it's terrible stuff, but it's alive and kicking in computer magazines right now.

So how do you say more or less the same thing, but differently? One way of doing so might be to produce a line reading: *'You get less for your money with a Damson home computer'*. The copy would then follow the 'less' theme, along the lines of: less memory restrictions, less difficult to operate, less of a hassle finding software, etc.

Taking it just one step further, we arrive at: *'Damson. . . Nobody gives you less'*.

Now, I would hold – and you may go along with me – that the 'less' story is rather more interesting than the 'more'. Agreed, it, too, is old hat, on account of I used it years ago; and probably not for the first time either. Yet it shows quite nicely that old ideas can be given new leases of life by a simple twist.

Generally speaking, therefore, don't be put off by the 'done before' accusation. Just so long as (a) you've rehashed the idea with some originality, and (b) you don't tear the fundament out of it.

We are supposed to be talking about headlines – so let's talk headlines. A headline, also widely called a concept, is one of the two devices you use to pull the reader into your limited sphere of operation. The other, obviously, is the illustration. Thus, you must first catch his attention, and then hold his interest long enough for him to absorb the full weight of your message.

The secret of attracting attention is that there is no secret. You cannot attract all of the people all of the time, and neither should you try. But what you must be at pains never to do is annoy, insult or upbraid a single one of them – whether they are in the market for what you're selling or not. Because one day they may be; and they'll remember as clearly as if it were yesterday that yours was the product which upset, offended or abused them. In which case, they won't touch it with a long pole.

I should not be at all surprised if there exists somewhere a set of statistics which proves beyond reasonable doubt that headlines enjoy two hundred per cent greater 'eye-value' than illustrations, and five hundred per cent greater readership than body copy. Nor, incidentally, should I be the least bit surprised (statistics being the malleable things they are) to learn that there is another set of them proving the converse.

I hold that all statistics, particularly those related to advertising, are as wide open to sober question as anything ever was.

It is obvious to anyone but a raving lunatic (whatever research may say) that, four times out of five, the headline is the most important single element in any advertisement. And if, not being a raving lunatic, you agree with me, you will give your headlines the attention they deserve – so that they, in their turn, will receive the attention they deserve.

What constitutes a deserving headline? There are, I believe, as many opinions on this as there are copywriters. But the general consensus appears to be that the best headlines will contain elements which (a) establish some kind of offer, (b) mention some immediate benefit of the product or service on offer, (c) name, or indicate price.

Most times, agreed, it's impossible to write a line that contains all three elements. It takes both talent and a product which lends itself to the use of the (I hate to say the word) formula.

Let's anyway decide that the majority of ads are better off for having a headline. This being so, surely that line should say something more than: 'Oi, I'm an advertisement'.

This may seem elementary to you, as indeed it does to me. But looking at the anguishing number of say-nothing phrases which masquerade as headlines betimes, it is quite apparent that our elementary lesson is far from having been universally learned.

Allow me to give you a few examples of headlines, gathered more or less at random, from recent general interest and technical magazines. It is, I know, unfair to quote them out of context with their supporting illustrations and copy. But I ask you to believe that, in none of the cases quoted, did either of these twin crutches prevent the headlines from falling flat on their faces.

1   *You pays your money, you takes your choice.*
2   *If you're looking for a xxxx, look no further.*
3   *You owe it to yourself.*
4   *There's never been a better time to buy a xxxxx.*
5   *Motorists don't know any better.*
6   *An open and shut case for xxxxx luggage.*
7   *When it comes to music centres, come to xxxxx.*

You may find them all pretty hard to believe, but I assure you they're true representations; and I will forebear to bore you with the three hundred others I have readily to hand.

Now these lines have one thing in common. They say absolutely nothing; and they offer likewise. Their empty platitudinizing, far from encouraging a prospect to dig a little more deeply into the ad, sends him scurrying for cover. What on earth do these ads think they are doing taking up good and valuable paid-for space? Worse, I know for a fact that some of them were put together under the auspices of agencies.

So you see, there is still plenty of room in the copywriting world for bright minds. Particularly if they have the happy knack of being able to find more interesting ways of presenting basically uninteresting propositions.

That's exactly what copywriters are overpaid to do.

To prove that I know roughly what I'm talking about, I propose here and now to contrive a basically uninteresting proposition and, with any luck, devise an attractive solution. (I realize that this could result in my downfall in your eyes, but I'll risk it.)

We'll take as the product, right off the top of the head, a common-or-garden photocopier. Our imaginary client is the main-dealer for a brand-name copier. He merchandizes these from half-a-dozen outlets in a given area. However, his competitors do exactly the same, in the same area, for various other top name copiers. For the sake of argument, let's call his product the Transcript Copier.

Now, to make things even more indifferent, the prices of Transcript are pegged by the manufacturer. So our man cannot bump the opposition by cutting prices. On top of that, the Transcript company does its own national advertising. Which means we are not pushing Transcript as a good buy per se, just as a good buy from our client – whom we shall call Bradley.

Pretty dreary stuff on the surface; though we've got to do something – so let's do something. By digging a little bit deeper, we discover that Bradley not only sells Transcript, but also makes a good living from the servicing of them. He does this on a contract basis by, we are told, a fairly competent team of his own engineers.

What about the market? It's made up of commercial and industrial people: office managers, accountants, architects, engineers, solicitors – you name it. But in my experience, the last thing they want to know about is photocopiers. Why? Well, office equipment is a very competitive growth industry; and our audience is bombarded with ads, mailers and phone calls of and about copiers nigh on every day of the week.

That's the brief – what do you make of it? What I make of it is this. 1 The first problem is to tell the market that Bradley sells the well-known Transcript copier. 2 We must inform them that Bradley is only too glad to turn out at any reasonable time to put things right in the unlikely event of a Transcript going wrong. 3 His unit prices and contract-maintenance prices are no cheaper than the next man's. His maintenance service may – just may – be somewhat more reliable. (That's what he tells us, anyway. But that's what they *all* tell us.)

As far as USPs go, Transcript doesn't have one. Neither, in all honesty, does Bradley; but we can get around it.

All right, let's put a few thoughts on paper. (Come on, you're in this, too.) Initially, we'd better jettison all the daft thoughts like: 'Taking out contracts on you' and 'We've got you covered'. Having done so, consider exactly what's implied in a maintenance contract. First, if you don't have one, you presumably either go in for do-it-yourself servicing, or call the nearest copier engineer and hope he doesn't keep you waiting for a fortnight before he turns up. Second, if you do have one, but one that isn't as good as it could be, you might just as well do-it-yourself.

So reflect on this: if you maintain the copier yourself, or have an indifferent servicing method, you'll very likely own a do-it-yourself manual. Nice thought; let's have a picture of a manual. Now for a line to go with it. What about:

IF YOU DON'T USE A TRANSCRIPT COPIER, YOU COULD PROBABLY USE THIS

A reasonable enough idea, but it would be better if we could imply that a Transcript needs less maintenance, thus suggesting that a Bradley maintenance contract works out cheaper. This, of course, would be spelled out in the body copy. So:

IS YOUR COPIER ENGINEER SPENDING MORE TIME ON IT THAN YOUR SECRETARY?

I'm not mad about it. In any case, there must be some way we can steal a march on the opposition by putting Bradley's name into the headline.

Therefore, let's have a go at:

IF YOUR SECRETARY COMPLAINS

ABOUT YOUR TRANSCRIPT SERVICING,

CHANGE TO BRADLEY

IF SHE STILL COMPLAINS

CHANGE YOUR SECRETARY

It will do at a pinch; and it says everything we want to say. It implies that Bradley gives a better service, and that he does so on Transcript. The copy will obviously reinforce the message; it will also stress his willingness to sell new copiers to whoever wants them.

Given that I had to come up with a couple of extra lines (just to show the client that I'm thinking on his behalf), I'd probably throw in something like this:

OUR TRANSCRIPT COPIERS COME WITH A

MAINTENANCE SERVICE THAT'S EVERY BIT AS

GOOD AS OUR TRANSCRIPT COPIERS

Or, like this:

NOBODY BUYS A TRANSCRIPT COPIER FOR

THE SAKE OF OUR MAINTENANCE SERVICE.

ESPECIALLY WHEN THEY'RE UNLIKELY TO

NEED IT!

I hope the example has transmitted some of the logic for arriving at the solution. If it hasn't, we could always try a further hypothetical exercise. Shall we? Very well.

* * *

This time, let's have a bash at recruitment advertising. The client, who is into electronics in a big way – we'll call him Ferrconi – has his plant slap in the nicest part of the Lake District. For that reason, oddly enough, he's having a modicum of trouble recruiting recently graduated, or low-experience engineers. They suppose they'll be going to a back-water and would far prefer to work in the steaming environs of a major city, where advancement might be more readily attained, and where salaries might be higher – they think.

As part of the brief, the client informs us that his firm undertakes substantial research work and has major contracts with the Ministry of Defence for producing missile guidance and avionics systems. He also pays well and the prospects for promotion are as good as can be found anywhere.

Our aim, as you can see, is to tell potential employees that Ferrconi is a good outfit for whom to work. After all, the MoD likes them; and there seems to be opportunity for creative experimentation.

I reckon there must be at least five hundred ways of solving this one. But, once again, let's ditch the nonsenses of: 'Ready for a brand new career?' and 'A switched-on job for electronics engineers' currently adorning the pages of the classier papers and specialist publications.

Where do we begin? We begin as always, with a rational-ization of Ferrconi's unique selling proposition. In this case, it's job opportunity, plus job satisfaction, plus the chance to live and work in Wordsworth country. Yes, I know recruits seem to prefer a metropolis, but they prefer a metropolis only because career advancement appears easier there. Can't we convince them that being top man in Ferrconi at £50,000 a year is far better than being second-fiddle at Marranti of London for the same money? Certainly, we can. Let's begin with a proposition that says:

GIVE US ONE MORE REASON WHY
YOU'D WANT TO WORK FOR FERRCONI

AND IT HAD BETTER BE GOOD

In this ad, we show illustrations of: 1 Scenery. 2 Fishing. 3 Golf. 4 Horse riding. 5 Sailing. We might even employ a squared-up blank space for the candidate's reasons.

Taking things a step further we could, using similar pictures, go for:

WORKING FOR FERRCONI IN THE
LAKE DISTRICT COULD BE THE END OF
CIVILIZATION AS YOU KNOW IT

The body copy, here, would hammer home the joys of a job in the Lake District, and how much more civilized it is to live there. Lots of variations on the above theme spring instantly to mind. But is it the right tack? I feel that it certainly isn't wrong, particularly if the copy grabs the open-air aspect by the throat.

For the purposes of this exercise, however, I am going to assume that Ferrconi won't let us major on the environment. They want ads, they say, which tell their hi-tech story in no uncertain terms; and in a way which will amuse young graduates.

Here, off the cuff, are several. Don't be put off by the length of the headlines, by the way. Long headlines, like body copy, will be read if they are *worth* reading. There's modesty for you. (I sincerely hope you're beavering away on this, too.)

IT TOOK TWO YEARS TO DISCOVER THAT HE
ISN'T CUT OUT FOR GUIDANCE SYSTEM
DESIGN

SO WE MADE HIM HEAD OF DEPARTMENT

(Picture: white-coated boffin in electronics situation.)

This one would say that young whatsisname proved to be too good to be a mere designer. It would also suggest that Ferrconi recognizes talent when it sees it. Next:

OUR TOP MISSILE GUIDANCE DESIGNER
SPENDS MOST OF HIS TIME PLAYING
SPACE INVADERS

(Picture: boffin studying computer-graphics screen.)

Our body copy on this offering talks at length about actual research programmes, plus the opportunities for making a big contribution to missile guidance work.

But wait, the client is back complaining that we haven't gone far enough to appeal to the fun-loving young characters they're hoping to attract. Oh, all right. What about this:

FERRCONI MISSILE GUIDANCE SYSTEMS
HOW ELSE DO YOU THINK E.T.
MADE IT HOME?

Alternatively:

WE'D LIKE YOU TO FIGURE OUT

HOW TO ZAP THE MEKON

BEFORE THE MEKON ZAPS US!

And:

WE CAN ALREADY HANDLE

STRANGE ENCOUNTERS OF

THE FIRST, SECOND AND

THIRD KIND.

WE'RE BUSY WORKING

ON THE FOURTH

Etc., etc. I presume you get the idea that just because the product is dull, the selling message needn't be likewise. And shouldn't be.

It seems to me that in a recruitment exercise of this kind, the company will receive any number of applications from people rather more fanciful than qualified. This being so, and simply to save much wasted interview time, what about including a technical test for the prospective candidates right in the ad?

A FREE GOLF/FISHING/GLIDING WEEKEND IN

THE LAKE DISTRICT FOR THE FIRST

CORRECT SOLUTION TO THIS PCB DESIGN

PROBLEM

*   *   *

I suggest we try one more – simply for the hell of it.

Car dealers all over the country are telling us what a rough time they are having of it lately. Imports, they say, are flooding the market. Unit prices are far too high – and British manufacturers refuse to allow them to do deals. And the money just isn't around for investment in new vehicles. More perturbingly, used car sales have dropped through the floor.

Our client, whom we shall call Bob Pride, owns a string of well-established garages in a large town; but he is one among many and his 'regulars' are casting around for higher trade-in offers. In the past, he has tried all of the gimmicks in an attempt to make sales – cheese-and-wine open nights, free in-car stereos, free petrol. Trouble is, his competitors are, or have been, on the same ineffective roundabout.

Aside from advising Mr Pride to sell up and retire gracefully to Rio, what can we do? Well, the curtain-raiser must be to ensure that he loses no more of his traditional customers. Second, we should try to endow him with an image which sets him apart from the rest. That is, as someone who has been around a long time, who values his reputation, and who won't wittingly let people down.

The latter proposal seems more a sop to Cerberus than a genuine effort to make sales.

Not so.

We all agree that standard motor-cars are the most unreliable and most carelessly-assembled items of machinery since the invention of the wheel – don't we? (If you don't, then we must simply put it down to my bad luck in these automotive things.) Realizing this, the buying public will clearly feel much happier knowing they have a friend in need.

But is he honest? Is he reliable? The best answer – and the only answer we are likely to get, if I know anything about it – is that he has a large servicing set-up, with wall-to-wall equipment and components, plus a team of time-served mechanics. Make of it what you will.

Here's my initial thought:

WE'VE ALL DONE BUSINESS WITH

INEFFICIENT GARAGES.

BUT NOT MUCH – AND NOT FOR LONG

Body copy would travel along the lines of: Our livelihood depends upon your custom. We want to keep you happy in every way we know how. Which is why we give you an after-sales service above and beyond the call of duty.

Not bad; but really not strong enough. On analysis, it strikes me as a 'so what', or a 'yeah, we've heard it all before' kind of ad. Then let's move on.

Presumably, the Pride organization goes in for some kind of corporate identity – possibly in the shape of a rear-windscreen sticker. If it doesn't, we recommend that it should. And thus:

WHEN WE PUT OUR NAME ON A CAR

IT STICKS

The illustration for this one could be a large, Bob Pride sticker; and the copy might say something to the effect of: Some garages put their stickers in cars purely because it's expected of them. Ours, by contrast, is there to prove that we are prepared to stand over every car we sell. So when we put a sticker in a car, we're not looking for free advertising. The car itself is the best advertisement we could wish.

Others in the same vein could say:

YOU CAN'T BUY

A BOB PRIDE STICKER

AT ANY PRICE

And:

IF YOU DON'T HAVE A BOB PRIDE STICKER

IN YOUR CAR,

NOW'S THE TIME TO JOIN THE AA

We may possibly suggest to the client that he actually offers AA membership to the first half-dozen non-Pride customers who apply. (He would, obviously, do the same for a given number of established customers.) I don't know whether the AA will go along with it or, indeed, know whether they can object – but think of the PR mileage if that organization agreed.

Or perhaps:

THE BUCK STOPS HERE

(Picture: Bob Pride himself in showroom or workshop situation.)

This one would declare that the customer is always right. In the event of problems, Mr Pride doesn't argue, doesn't quibble, makes no excuses. He just puts things right – instantly. That way, customers remain customers; and the garage remains one of the finest dealers in the country.

It's crude and it's an old trick, Biggles; but it just might work.

Looking specifically at the used car side of the business, how about a mildly negative approach?

BOB PRIDE'S USED CARS

ARE PASSED IT

In the meat of this ad, we would employ a series of official-looking 'passed' stamps. Therefore:

Mechanical soundness   PASSED
Upholstery   PASSED
Bodywork   PASSED
Twelve-month warranty PASSED

It strikes me that we should also develop a good, strong 'umbrella' line to appear as a tag on all used car ads. Knowing that garages are awarded new-car dealerships by manufacturers, what's to stop us suggesting that Pride has a similar type of distributorship for *used cars?* He's an appointed used-car dealer, if you like. How do we do it? Like this:

BOB PRIDE.

YOUR USED CAR MAIN DEALER

It's a beauty. Can't you just picture the indignant reactions of all the other used car dealers in the area? They will be hopping mad; and they will be firing off writs in all directions. But their lawyers will be fruitlessly employed, since there's nothing whatsoever illegal in the sentiments of the line. A touch crafty, even a whit amoral – but certainly not dishonest.

How can I be so sure? As it happens, I wrote the line a while ago for a car-dealer client. The response and the outcome was as given above, with the exception that my chap was actually buying-in used cars in order to satisfy the demand.

*   *   *

If you'll allow me, I should like to deviate for a moment and say a word or two about headline and copy layout from the copywriter's point of view. Innumerable writers – including some of the best – are to typing what lockjaw is to conversation. Hopeless. This in itself is allowable; but many of them seem to have little regard for the appearance of what they write, which isn't. Their ideas may be admirable, yet the way they present them is criminal. Headlines are typed as one long, single line right across the page, with no thought for the reader, i.e. the visualizer/designer/account executive/client. And body copy is literally chucked on to the paper – the words often scampering over the edge like typographical lemmings.

To my simple mind, this is laziness well carried out. I refute absolutely the notion that such is the inevitable side-effect of an artistic temperament. Moreover, as I've said, it helps nobody – including the typographer and, now and again, the compositor.

If you, the writer, neglect to balance your headlines on the typed page, decline to break lines at natural pauses, omit to show where the second or third clauses, or elements, begin and end, don't be at all surprised if the finished ad fails to scan.

During the typing of a line, I've often found better ways of phrasing it simply from the look of the thing. Ambiguity, for instance, and clumsy phrasing, shows up as the words go down. It therefore pays to put it on paper the way you wish to see it in print.

Now and again, I go one step farther and scribble a rough layout for a given ad. Unarguably, one should have a good relationship with the visualizer before presuming to move into the recondite world of design, otherwise you risk derision at best, or a black eye at worst. I should also stress that these scribbles, which are no more than 'thumbnails', are for my benefit alone and are for the purpose of assessing the look of the words once they hit the page. Similarly, I can assess exactly how much or how little I can get away with.

Take an idea for a prestige ad for a construction company which has undertaken a massive building programme on, say, the island of Orkney. The programme cost £70 million and took ten years to complete. For whatever reason, we are given a double-page spread to do the job. However, no pictures or illustrations are available. So we have a lot of space and very little to put into it. What we do have, though, is a list of twelve building projects and their individual costs.

In which case, I might write:

Left-hand page

THIS LIST REPRESENTS £70,000,000-WORTH
OF BUILDING PROJECTS
UNDERTAKEN IN THE ORKNEYS
IN THE LAST TEN YEARS

Kirkwall Civic Centre   £3,500,000
(Plus 11 more)

Right-hand page

THIS LIST REPRESENTS
THE COMPANIES RESPONSIBLE

Charterhouse Construction Limited
(Logo/Address/Telephone)

Building Design · Civil Engineering · Project Management
Site Management · Plant Hire · Building Construction

Like that it looks quite a mess – but like this, it doesn't:

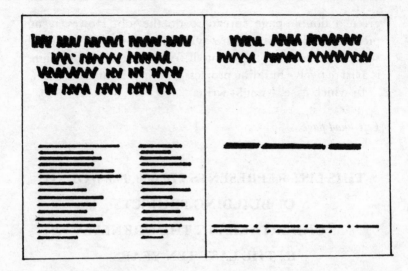

And that's headline writing in a nutshell. If nothing else, the foregoing should at least give you an insight into the thinking behind concept work.

Rule 9   *Every headline should be the best you've ever written.*

You're only as good as your last ad is an axiom that copywriters hear all too often. And it happens to be true. But there is a positive side to it. If you can ensure that every ad you put together stands firmly on its own two feet, then the last ad always maintains your reputation. Good writers are rarely happy with their work; and never complacent. Yet that does not preclude you from being proud of it – does it?

Summary

1   Never, ever go along with the first headline that comes your way. In some cases, as I'm forced to agree, you may well revert to the line you originally thought of on account of the fact that everything subsequently written

failed to come up to scratch. But explore all avenues before making a final choice. All avenues in this case means writing at least two-dozen lines to eventually arrive at one.

2   Devising a headline is comparable to inventing a better mousetrap. You often end up with something so contrived, so complicated, that it is lost on everyone – including the mouse. Headlines don't have to be short to be sharp. (There have been ads – many of them excellent – in which the entire piece consisted of nothing but a very long, bold headline. And I mean fifty, sixty, seventy words or more.) Whether these can strictly be called headlines, or whether they are body copy writ bold, I don't know. But they can be effective.

Nor, indeed, need they be clever or witty to be apt. However, the one characteristic they must possess, above all, is attractiveness. Now, it can be argued that attractiveness is strictly in the eye of the beholder; and what engages one reader may well turn out to be repellent to another – even when both appear to have identical tastes and interests.

Consider, for a moment, the following lines. I ask you to imagine that each is accompanied by a picture of the sitting-room of a luxury flat, in which a modishly-dressed young man is entertaining a young woman – or, indeed, the other way about.

(a)   *Lansdowne Luxury Flats. Interior design by René. Environment by Catherine's Wharf. Social status by implication.*

(b)   *Will a Lansdowne Luxury Flat attract disturbingly beautiful people and dramatically affect your love life?*

Both are for the same well-appointed, trendily-decorated (and fictitious) pad. Both are aimed at young men and women who are several rungs up the executive ladder. But neither one, I venture to suggest, will appeal to the sensibilities of the person implied in the structure of the other. Both lines express the same sentiments, more or less; yet they are petitioning manifestly different characters. Nothing to do with up-market or down-market, since both subjects are well-heeled. They're just psychologically different. Number one responds to snob-appeal, while number two likes to be titillated.

Awareness of these fractional differences in a given market is not merely desirable, it's mandatory. Knowing how to reach each is likewise.

7   Copy proper

Perhaps it's time we went into copy in depth. Very well, I now propose to talk about copy construction – phrasing and style. Then we'll set ourselves a few hypothetical briefs and write sufficient copy to satisfy them. Later in the chapter, I'll devise some extra, chimerical briefs, but without providing immediate answers to them. This ought to give you a good opportunity to try out what you've picked up. My own efforts appear towards the end of the book.

Are you on? Fine.

In constructing copy, you are at liberty to take liberties with the language. Sentences need not be true sentences in the grammatical sense. Just so long as they communicate, it matters not what you call them. Get used to writing short, sharp sentences (non-noun clauses, if you like – you'll see what I mean shortly) consisting of the absolute minimum of words. Because the shorter and punchier the elements, the easier they are to absorb, and the more powerful the message.

As a for instance, here's what an uninitiated electronics expert suggested we should say about his latest brain-child – a microcomputer for the home – in a popular computer magazine:

The new X-45 home computer is endowed with a 64K bytes

memory and employs the very latest techniques in MSX, omni-language technology. Moreover, the MSX feature allows infinite and on-going interchangeability of programs, cassettes and even peripherals, such as disk-drives and joy-sticks, with other machines. . . .

I strongly suspect that even a computer wizard, up to his eyes in bytes and joy-sticks, would find that little lot pretty hard going.

Now here's what we did for the re-write:

Meet the X45 home computer. It's got a big 64K memory. And one-language MSX.

So you can trade programs and cassettes with any other MSX.

You can do the same with disk-drives and joy-sticks, too. . . .

Note that the sentences are technically clauses which have been given sentence status. To write in this fashion, all you have to do is find a natural break in a given sentence – one that would normally be indicated by a comma – and drop in a full-point instead.

The idea, as we've said, is to write easy-on-the-eye material that will be rapidly digested.

All ads start life with the same basic problem; the audience has little or no interest in reading them. On top of that, they have to overcome the clamorous opposition of dozens more ads in the same publication. Furthermore, an ad has a limited amount of space in which to express itself. (Even a full-page space is a limited space.) This is no real problem for the professional writer. He will deliver the message no matter how small the allocated space. The real secret is self-discipline and economy of words.

How are these attributes achieved? Only one way: by constant practice. In the early days, everything you produce will be far too long. Thus, you must go through the work and edit unmercifully – cut every extraneous thought, delete every irrelevant word – until the piece is reduced to manageable and useable proportions. That done, you should write a second version; the difference being in the phrasing, rather than in the product detail. Now compare the two. You will see that bits of the first sit more comfortably in the second, and per contra. So the answer is to knock out a third piece, using the best lines from both. After a while, your material will transmute into the concise and precise, highly-polished style of the professional. Eventually, you'll be able to omit the intermediate stage altogether; and your first attempt, plus a polish, will be sufficient for each job.

But as I've implied, practice along with total application is the only road to travel. Developing a style doesn't happen overnight; arriving at a point where people recognize your work by style alone – and not because they know which accounts you handle – takes working at. Lonely, frustrating work at that.

I digress. So now, the mechanics of copy and some techniques for putting it together – stage by stage. In the following exercise, my interjections between the actual copy elements are *not* part of a magic formula. They are there as guidelines only.

As the hub for this exercise, we'll contrive the launch of a new estate-car called the Viking GL. Its selling points, in order of importance, are:

1   Measurably, a larger interior capacity than any other estate vehicle on the market. We shall make it three cubic feet larger.
2   The fuel consumption is comparable with that of a small car: 45 m.p.g.
3   When compared to other cars of its size and class, the Viking works out at average cost – say, £5000.

Some car.

I am suggesting that a headline has already been written for this project. For better or worse, it says:

LOAD HOG!

Hopefully, the line speaks for itself; but whatever your reservations, it does us the undoubted service of telling the big-capacity story fairly crisply. How original it is, I don't know. What's more, I think the exclamation mark is well justified in this case.

All right, the first step is to establish the name of the vehicle – to make certain everyone knows what we're talking about:

Introducing the new Viking GL. The load hog.

Followed by a brief description:

A cleverly designed estate-car that's bigger on space. Easier on petrol.

And a reinforcement of its major USP:

In fact, the Viking GL gives you more interior space than any other estate currently on the market.
A full three cubic feet more.

With the customer benefit:

So there's loads more room for passengers.
Loads more room for luggage. And loads more room for loads more.

Now we cover the remaining selling points:

But, remarkably, it costs no more than an ordinary estate-car.
Running economy? Outstanding.
Even fully loaded, you can expect – and get – an impressive 45 miles to every gallon.

Just as impressive is the price. £5000 is all.
Not a lot to pay for what you get.

At this point, we may be required to give some technical
detail about steering, braking, road-holding, etc. But we will
do that only if forced – because there will be, or should be,
reams of manufacturer's literature for the punter to get his
hands on. One way of avoiding the penning of acres of facts
and figures is to make comparisons, where possible, with
other, previously launched Viking models. In which case,
we'd say something to the effect of: *The Viking GL estate has the*
same superb steering, braking and road-holding qualities as the tried-
and-tested Viking saloons. Positive, safe and completely reliable. Not
much more, though.

Finally, we need a pay-off. Something to galvanize the
reader into viewing the Viking at close quarters. So:

Why not find out more? And if you like what you see,
take a test-drive.
Your local Viking dealer has all the facts and all the
figures.
Or call this number. We'll arrange that test-run at
your home.

You may feel that we require a final statement which sums
up the vehicle in concise terms. This line should major
specifically on the capacity story, yet still suggest that its size
is no hindrance to handleability. What about:

The Viking GL. Drives like a car – loads like a van.

As you see, the copy developed naturally by: (a) linking the
first line with the headline, (b) spelling out, early on, the
attributes of the vehicle, (c) reinforcing those benefits with
capacity/price/economy facts, (d) urging the prospect to
take some positive action.

Additional points to note are: (e) each USP was mentioned, or hinted at, twice, (f) the employment of some simply-

phrased questions to open doors to sales points, (g) tight paragraphs are easy to scan.

A two-word question like 'How come?', for instance, is an effective and neat device for linking a promise with the facts about that promise. Take the following promise: 'We give you a better service than most'. If followed by 'How come?' can help us introduce factual evidence like: 'Our service engineers are on call twenty-four hours a day,' or whatever the case happens to be.

I'll repeat what I said earlier. Keep it short and keep it simple. Much copy has no more than single-sentence paragraphs. Often, just one word suffices as a sentence. But only constant use – meaning constant trial and error – will get you to that level of skill.

As a decent-sized ad in one of the nationals, the above copy and headline, along with a suitable illustration (perhaps a picture of the number of people, plus the amount of luggage and paraphernalia which may be carried), would be quite impressive. The moderate length of the copy lends itself to the use of a large typeface; and that will make it the more readable.

Although you may probably never need to know anything about typefaces or typesizes, you should be aware that type is measured in 'points'. There are twelve points to an 'em' and six ems, or seventy-two points, to the inch. The type you are reading is eleven point. That much is worth knowing, because when your designer says he intends putting a headline in forty-eight point, you won't be left with a blank expression. Will you?

The above ad would also work, relatively speaking, in an A4-size magazine, either as a full page or a half-page. All that happens in this case is that the picture and/or the typesize is reduced in proportion.

* * *

Enough of that. We have just picked up a new client. He is in the middle-of-the-road furniture business. By that, I am not suggesting he retails junk; but neither does he stock the thoroughbreds of the furniture world, either. He also sells bed-linen, carpets and curtains; and his outlets are in the shape of three, well-established, well-appointed high-street department stores.

From what is known of his market, we recommend full pages in the local press. (Not all local papers are tin-pot and hastily put together rags. Some are every bit as good as the nationals.) His main competitors, since his is a traditional business, are the new crop of furniture warehouses springing up in his area. These tend to offer very little in the way of personal service and operate, as we know, on a take-it-or-leave-it basis. Our man, on the other hand, prides himself on his customer-relations.

That's the brief. Out of it comes the deduction that our job is to woo the middle-market furniture buyers back to the traditional shop; and back to our client's traditional shop for preference. Which gives us our first lead: knock the warehouses. But we'll knock them gently – we don't want our chap (we shall call him Smith & Jones Ltd) to appear mealy-mouthed.

One way of cracking it would be this way:

WHEN YOU BUY FURNITURE

FROM WAREHOUSES,

YOU GET WAREHOUSE FURNITURE

Too obscure? Maybe. But let's see if a touch of copy can bale us out.

The word warehouse sends shivers up our spine.

Not that we're troubled by the opposition. Far from it.

What does trouble us is the sad quality of the goods you get for your money.

And the service you don't get.

No – that way lies trouble. We're leaving ourselves wide open for a public argument. We can still be as strong – even stronger – if we stay away from direct attacks. Like this:

THE REASON WE DON'T SELL

CHEAP FURNITURE

IS THAT IT'S LIABLE TO BE

EXPENSIVE

Five hundred per cent better, if you ask me. And the first line of copy says it all:

We don't sell you cheap. But neither will we sell you short.

It would continue thus:

Because our reputation is more valuable than a quick sale.

Our philosophy is to sell well-made, attractive furniture at an honest price.

And to give paying customers the service they richly deserve. Take-it-or-leave-it isn't our way of doing business.

But if you don't buy on this occasion, we know you'll be back sometime.

Even if it's only because you enjoy being called 'sir' or 'madam'.

Of course, we'd use pictures of the furniture, along with descriptions and pricetags. It strike me, too, that the headline works well, once adapted, for the curtains, carpets and so on.

THE REASON WE DON'T SELL
CHEAP CARPETS IS THAT THEY'RE
LIABLE TO BE EXPENSIVE

What about a pay-off? One that tells both the service and the civilized shopping story. Something in this area looks apt:

Smith & Jones. For an old-fashioned thing called service.

* * *

That's far enough on furniture. We've another new client eager to see what we can do for him. He happens to be the chairman of a committee of fitted kitchen manufacturers. These people are unhappy about the state of the trade. It has a bad reputation for shoddy workmanship; for jacking up the quoted price in the middle of a job; and for going bust without warning – with customers' deposits tucked away in their banks.

Quite sensibly, the committee has set up a kind of consumer protection (trade protection?) organization, consisting of a number of selected firms. The organization backs their work and bails them out in the event of financial problems.

What we have been asked to do is tell those potential fitted kitchen customers, via the national press, that 1 The organization exists, and 2 That it undertakes to be a guarantor of good workmanship and fair-play.

Who are they? The Kitchen Specialists Association. How shall we tackle it. Well, we can be as forthright as we wish. The only people we are likely to upset are the bad lads.

THIS NEW CONSUMER PROTECTION
ORGANIZATION WAS FORMED BY
A BUNCH OF COWBOYS

That line may be a little too rich for the client's blood. We'll tone it down somewhat.

WE'RE HERE TO STOP THINGS
BOILING OVER
IN YOUR KITCHEN

All right, take your choice. Now let's progress through the copy. First, an opener to suggest that we have sympathy for the customer:

> *When you employ a firm to install your new fitted kitchen, you expect them to do exactly that.*
> *You don't need excuses about availability of parts. You don't want them to put up the price half-way through.*
> *You certainly don't expect them to go bust at your considerable expense.*

Wait for it:

> *In short, you don't need cowboys.*

And now for the service:

> *Which is why we've formed the KSA. The Kitchen Specialists Association.*
> *An organization specially set up to protect your interests.*
> *Our members are carefully vetted. We accept only those with a record of good workmanship and fair dealing.*

The USP:

> *Better still, in the unlikely event of problems, we step in to sort things out on your behalf.*
>   *So the very next time you talk to someone about a fitted kitchen, make sure he's a member of the KSA.*
>   *Or give us a call for our approved list.*
>   *That way, you won't get bushwhacked!*

> *KSA (logo)*
> *Address/Telephone*

The possibilities, here, for good puns are practically endless. Thus, you may wish to perform some wordplay around kitchens.

WITHOUT KSA YOUR KITCHEN CABINETS

COULD HAVE ONE MORE CATCH

THAN YOU BARGAINED FOR

Now, it may just happen that the client also wants to run an ad which recruits fitted kitchen specialists into his organization. In that event, the approach must obviously be different – though none the less authoritative:

IF YOU CAN'T STAND

THE HEAT

STAY OUT OF THE KITCHEN

Plus copy that says:

> *That's what we tell firms who apply to join our organization.*
>   *The Kitchen Specialists Association.*
>   *We're here to monitor the work of fitted kitchen craftsmen.*

*And to help them make a better name for themselves.
It's good for the industry. It's good for your
customers. It's good for you.*

And so forth.

* * *

To change the subject somewhat – and in order to furnish as
diverse a set of examples as possible in this chapter – let us
now ponder the problems of promoting the legal profession.
You'll be aware that in 1984 (1985 in Scotland) the Law
Society gave the go-ahead for its members to advertise.
Quite a few solicitors were dead against it, their opinions
formed, doubtlessly, by what they had seen their American
cousins perpetrating – ten-dollar divorces and all. But some
were for it.

Anyway, the launching of solicitors was fraught with
difficulties. The strict, and restricting, guidelines laid down
by the Law Society had to be adhered to; as did those of the
advertising watchdogs which already pertained. On top of
that, those solicitors who were prepared to advertise brought
with them the classic inhibitions derived from hundreds of
years of conforming to unwritten, but none the less tangible,
codes of practice.

Once I had read the literature and listened to the
arguments, I concluded that it boiled down to just three
criteria. 1 In any written or verbal promotion, a solicitor
could not suggest that he was any better – any more efficient,
any cheaper, any more knowledgeable – than any other
solicitor. 2 Ludicrously, he could not directly solicit
business. Meaning that in any advertising he had to promote
the broad concept of the desirability of employing a solicitor,
rather than promote himself specifically. 3 Solicitors, like
Caesar's wife, had to be above suspicion of cutting rates, of
'being in the know', or of claiming efficacy in any particular
field. So exhortations like: 'We're just the boys to get you off

that charge of indecent exposure', whether or not the said
boys were the undisputed saviours of people given to
indecently exposing themselves, were not on.

All of which left one wondering whether it was worth the
effort. As you've no doubt guessed, though, the Law Society
– not being mugs in any respect – spun enough loopholes to
allow any copywriter who was not a complete moron to leap
through the net and thumb his nose from the other side.
(With no loopholes to dive into, both the copywriter and the
solicitor would have to turn respectable. Then where would
they be?)

If this were not bad enough, there were even more
constraints to take into the reckoning. In marketing the
services of a solicitor for the first time, how do you go into the
marketplace without alienating the firm's traditional,
conservatively-minded clients? Conversely, how do you
approach the younger, less conventional segment in a
language it understands? In effect, in language that doesn't
sound like a direct lift from an erudite treatise on the Laws of
Tort?

Whatever was produced had to be acceptable to the
traditionalists, who already knew all about solicitors anyway, and informative to the up-and-coming, who very likely
didn't.

Give or take several dozen closely-typed pages – plus the
information that the client's firm is called Gray, Robertson
& Wilkie – that's the brief as I received it. The initial aim
was to put together one large launch ad, one slightly smaller
follow-up ad, and three or four reminders around half the
size of the launch piece.

Are you able to resolve it – or shall I assist? Oh, very well
then.

Ladies and gentlemen, we require a tag-line; a device we
can plaster on every bit of promotional material; a word or
two which sums up our client as a knowledgeable, respectable practitioner who knows the law, can arrange

mortgages, will represent you in court, draws up wills, and does the necessary when you are buying or selling a house.

Did I say it was going to be easy?

Since your first solicitor is likely to be your last, if you follow me, I would suggest something like: 'A friend in need', or 'A friend for life'. Though seeing as how the latter could so easily be misread, or mis-printed, as 'A fiend for life', its use may be considered hazardous. Better still, I would propose:

YOUR LEARNED FRIENDS

Why don't we put those three words into a circle and 'stamp' it on everything? What a good idea.

Now for a headline for the launch ad; a headline that presents a rational case for our solicitor; one that gives good reason for his name being splashed all over the papers.

Will you go along with this:

AT LONG LAST,
WE CAN NOW PREACH
WHAT WE PRACTISE

And go into the copy – restrained, but eager to show our man's existing clients that he has not fallen off his trolley.

We honestly don't believe that advertising will lower the tone of the legal profession.

That's our considered opinion and if they don't like it . . . we'll water it down a bit:

It certainly won't lower the professional standards of this particular firm.

And we believe advertising to be a good thing. For these reasons.

Now gently into enlightening the uninitiated market:

1 We can now talk openly about our services.

2 **We can say that our advice and assistance won't cost the earth.**
3 **We can tell you that our knowledgeable team will give you its undivided attention on a wide range of matters.**

Plus a rough outline of the services offered:

4 **Like: house sale and purchase. Will-making. Unfair dismissal. Business partnerships. Legal aid. Criminal injuries. Mortgages.**
5 **All of which will be handled strictly within our Professional Code of Conduct. By people dedicated to helping you.**

Finally, we attempt to reassure the established clients.

There, that didn't hurt a bit – did it?
GRW (logo)
Address/Telephone
Your Learned Friends

I see that one as an all-type ad – no illustration. Also, it should be set in a classic typeface, with the 1 to 5 figures picked out in bold and at least three sizes larger than the body-copy type. This should give the ad the look of an 'official communication'.

In the follow-up ad, we can afford to be less defensive. Within the restraints mentioned earlier, we can now push the client's services right to the fore. Here, too, we might seriously consider employing the sentiments of our tag-line as a constituent of the headline. What we can't do, as you've seen, is say anything to the effect of: 'If you're in trouble, have a word with Your Learned Friends', because learned friends in this context is Gray, Robertson and Wilkie. So let's do it by implication – using learned friends as a generic term for all solicitors.

WHEN IN DOUBT,

TURN TO A LEARNED FRIEND

This now gives us the licence to name our client in the copy, without his appearing to be pushing a specific skill.

> *When they need help, most people turn to a friend.*
> *A knowledgeable friend.*
> *Someone whose opinion they value.*
> *And that's exactly what you'll find at Gray, Robert-*
> *son and Wilkie.*

Now that everyone knows who we are talking about, we outline his services – which, quite obviously, could be claimed by any solicitor:

> *Our knowledgeable team can provide advice, and very*
> *real assistance, on a wide variety of legal matters.*
> *From house sale and purchase. To drawing up a*
> *will.*
> *From representation in court. To settling a dispute*
> *with a neighbour.*
> *From arranging a mortgage. To drawing up*
> *business partnership agreements.*

Plus a kicker for those who may not be able to afford a solicitor:

> *And if you qualify for Legal Aid, our services are*
> *absolutely free.*

And the pay-off:

> *So when you're in any doubt at all, turn to a learned*
> *friend.*
> *GRW (logo)*
> *Address/Telephone*
> *Your Learned Friends*

As far as I know, this copy sticks to the letter of the Law Society law – just. Yet there's little doubt that a good prosecuting barrister could take it apart comma by comma and prove me embarrassingly wrong. One must accept these things; but I have a special plea which should make interesting reading once reporting restrictions are lifted. The client is a solicitor and I took his advice on all matters.

Talking of whom – what about the smaller reminder ads? And why shouldn't we have some fun with these?

Picture the following. The ad space is 15 cm × 3 columns. We shall make three. Each contains a pithy headline; and each accommodates a tasteful cartoon illustration that directly contradicts the headline. The message I'm striving to project in these is: 'Far be it from us to say we told you so, but we told you so'.

Ad number one, then, consists of an illustration of a frustrated-looking chap who is pictured up to his eyebrows in law tomes. We can distinguish the titles: Law Made Easy, Simple Conveyancing, Sale of Goods Act, Criminal Injuries for Beginners; Partnership Law – and so on. The headline reads:

WHAT CAN WE TELL YOU

THAT YOUR COMMON SENSE CAN'T?

Number two shows a dispirited convict in a prison cell, complete with an arrowed-suit and ball-and-chain.

IT'S A WATERTIGHT CASE,

I SHALL DEFEND MYSELF

Number three is a cameo of a major road-works, or multistorey car park, being driven through, or erected in, the perplexed subject's front garden. Said subject is arguing fiercely with the foreman of the construction squad.

ANY FOOL CAN HANDLE HIS OWN

CONVEYANCING . . .

AND QUITE A FEW DO

In all of these, I see only three or four lines of copy; and maybe the same copy for each:

Don't go it alone, you'll almost certainly lose.
Have a word with a solicitor. Have a word with your learned friends.

Plus, of course, the logo and the address, phone and tag lines. If we can get away with it, which is most unlikely, I should also put up a special, one-off Christmas ad. It features Santa Claus and his reindeer-drawn sleigh in collision with a car. The motorist is unperturbed and smiling.

I NEED A LAWYER

LIKE A MOOSE

NEEDS A HATRACK

Plus a soupcon of copy:

Nobody will believe him when he makes his insurance claim.
Santa driving with undue care and attention? Never!
Witnesses? What witnesses?
Don't go it alone. You'll almost certainly lose.

And so forth.

*   *   *

Just to make sure the foregoing has sunk in, let's do a few final headline/copy concept exercises. But this time you're on your own – you get the brief only. I am asking you to pen your ideas based on that brief, along with several lines of introduction copy (we've got to know how you'll develop the headlines, haven't we?) My solutions to the problems are found in Chapter 12. I urge you not to look at them until you are happy with your own efforts. Fat chance of that, eh?

With any luck, and if I've done my job properly, we should be pretty much in agreement on the tack to take. Are you ready?

Exercise 1

This time the brief is from an electronics company that makes portable typewriters, mini-photocopying machines, and small computers. Each of these products is produced specifically for the home-user, or the small businessman.

I'll take the typewriter first. This model – the Z60 – is the first cordless portable on the market. It has a choice of typestyles, a fifteen-character visual display and one-line memory feature (so you can see what you have typed long before it goes on the paper). Finally, it costs £190.

With this product, we're aiming at people who (a) work from home and, (b) travel around and need a go-anywhere typewriter.

The ads will appear in the national press and national periodicals: *Radio Times* etc. Our market is anyone likely to own a typewriter – small businesses, aspiring novelists, freelance journalists and such like.

Away you go then.

Exercise 2

Now for the photocopiers. They're smaller than average. Lighter than average. (Dimensions: 20 × 20 × 8 in. Weight:

7 lbs 11 oz.) But are capable of producing 2000 copies at one loading. Further, they will copy on to any type or weight of paper and reproduce in a range of five colours. We'll call it the Vulcan 10 copier.

The Vulcan 10 is produced particularly for smaller businesses. In that respect, our media will be fairly selective. National press, yes – but we'll be using the more up-market papers. At least, the picture papers are out. In addition, our ads will also appear in trade magazines like *Business & Finance, The Accountant, Architects Journal* and so forth.

Is that sufficient?

Exercise 3

Finally, in the office equipment section, we move on to the minicomputers. The brief informs us that the product – the Cogent II – is a pocket-size machine, rather like a calculator, but with a memory comparable to a full-scale, personal computer (well, it could happen, and perhaps much sooner than we think). This machine is designed to help with the balancing of books, stock control, sales and profit projections and invoicing. It can be plugged into any TV screen for visual display: i.e. twenty-four lines by ninety characters per line. And when connected to a compatible printer, it will print out anything stored in the 64K memory.

Most importantly, the Cogent II costs about half the price of a conventional computer.

The market, once again, is the small business. And the media will be approximately as for the photocopier above.

Exercise 4

Now for something completely different.

A national passenger coach operator is taking a hiding

from the competition of British Rail and, to a lesser extent, from the internal airlines. Specifically, his regular London to Edinburgh schedule is suffering. The train makes the trip some four hours faster, while the air-shuttle beats him by a clear eight hours.

What does he have to offer to compensate? In the first place, his single, London to Edinburgh fare is £11. By train, the cost is £35 and air-fare works out at £95 one way. (His return fare is £22.)

So he's considerably cheaper.

Next, he operates the route twice a day, every day, using super-luxury coaches which make passenger stops through-out the London/Edinburgh suburbs – in and out. The coaches have reclining seats, personal lighting and heating systems, and plenty of leg-room.

The major drawback is the nine solid hours of travelling involved.

Our market appears to be: students, low-ranking service-men, and middle-to-low income groups generally.

For the sake of this exercise, we are handling the London end of things only. In which case, the media will be local London papers and London editions of the nationals.

I suppose we had better give this company a name. How about Trans-National Coaches? Good idea.

* * *

Before you give all of that a whirl, maybe a small tip is in order. Some copywriters are methodical. Some aren't. Many carry all the ingredients of a brief in their heads and work extempore, so to speak. Many can't. If you're among the latter, it will help if you note the various points under a series of headings. Taking the case of the Z60 typewriter mentioned earlier, a briefing aid will look something like the chart below.

A word about the layout of typed copy. There are many

schools of thought; and a dozen different house-styles. For myself, I prefer the headline to be typed in upper and lower-case and underlined. This gives the designer a better idea of where *necessary* caps fall. Since if you type the entire line in caps and he wants to run it in upper and lower for the finished ad, he may capitalize the wrong words. I've seen it happen. As for the body copy, I personally don't indent for new paragraphs, but use additional line-space to indicate paragraphs. But, like I say, it's a matter of individual choice.

So how did you fare with the exercises? Tolerably well? I'm glad.

Simple briefing aid

Products	USPs		Benefits	Media	Price	Market
Z60	1	First ever cordless electronic typewriter	1 Will operate anywhere	National press	£190	Freelance writers
	2	Compact and lightweight	2 Easy to transport			Smaller businesses
	3	Choice of typefaces	3 Allows various presentation styles			Home use
	4	Visual display of fifteen characters	4 Helps prevent typing errors			
	5	One-line memory	5 Allows editing			

Summary

1   What is it that makes one ad pull punters with the energy of a Sunday-morning bell-ringer, while another ad – in

the same publication, of the same size, couched in roughly the same terms – pulls nothing but disinterested glances? Well, if you knew the answer you'd be a very wealthy person indeed; and the last thing you'd be doing is pondering silly questions like this. But as daft as it may seem, it's not such an idiotic question that thousands of people haven't spent half their lives trying to resolve it.

I often wonder how many thousands of hours and trillions of words have been expended on explaining to insensitive clients that nobody knows, or is even likely to know, the answer. When this is pointed out to them – usually slowly, in words of one syllable – they adopt a disbelieving stance. One cannot blame them. It must be difficult to lash out good money on what is, after all, a never-conclusive experiment.

The best we can do, therefore, in the preparation of ads is present a handsome-looking, coherently-worded creation and hope that it has charisma enough to get itself noticed wherever and whenever it appears. More-over, it has to be an attractive package wherein the gift, once unwrapped, does not come as an anti-climax. The headline, the picture and the copy must weld as one harmonious unit.

There is very little worse than a headline that promises the earth, sitting above concomitant copy that delivers only half a spadeful of stony soil.

In my younger days, with wild and, as it turned out, unrequited enthusiasm, I chased a girl who was the daughter of a tycoon. In order to impress, I used to put my barely-afforded Woodbines into a Dunhill tin (or was it Balkan Sobranie?), and mighty impressive I felt. The girl, in the event, escaped; but it occurs to me that maybe the tin wasn't to blame. Maybe, just maybe, it was that the tin offered what I had no hope of furnishing, and the girl (or, more likely, her father) got the penurious message.

The message, then, is write the whole ad as an entire unit. Writing 'stopper' headlines is a superb idea – just so long as you follow it up with a 'goer' of a proposition.

8   Setting a good example

The following illustrations are examples of what advertising is, or should be, all about. They may not be the trendiest or, indeed, the slickest pieces of work ever to appear in print. But, to my mind, they succeed in their intentions. Each has a certain compulsive style; and from what I can gather, they did what they were paid to do. They were seen, read and acted upon. And when all is said and done, *that* is what advertising is all about.

Figures 1, 2 and 3   Three ads from a superb series by the legendary J. Walter Thompson (London) agency for the British Pharmaceutical Industry. A classic example of the true 'campaign'; and designed and written with thorough-bred panache.

Figures 4 and 5   These two could almost be stills from a Hitchcock movie – attractive and sinister at one and the same time. And the McGuffin is in there, too. A couple of very crisp ads by Covey Advertising (Edinburgh). Is the girl justified in this case? Certainly.

Figures 6 and 7   Energetic, eye-catching cartoons tempered by well thought-out copy give these Geers Gross

(London) ads a touch of attention-getting class. It's a combination that must have had Telecom's phones permanently engaged.

Figure 8   Twenty words which graphically prove that 'no copy' ads can take a genuine selling role. Anything more in this highly emotive piece would have been totally redundant.

Figure 9   Equal proof that 'long' copy does have a place. And by the time you reach the end of it, you'll not only be an authority on the evils of booze, but also a lot wiser about how to tell a basically dreary story very interestingly. (Both by Halls Advertising – Edinburgh.)

Figure 10   Nobody in the catering trade could possibly have seen this satanic picture and 'you've been warned' headline without experiencing just a twinge of apprehension. The ad, by Allen, Brady & Marsh (London), shows that an ad doesn't need to scream its head off to be powerful.

Figures 11 and 12   Here's the art of copywriting in a nutshell. Produced by the Bill Hopkins/Joe Baker partnership more than a dozen years ago, these two ads are still as fresh as the day they were born.
  Polished copy, excellent illustrations – consummate ads. Two very interesting nutshells, wouldn't you say?

Figure 13   Part of the Flexilink campaign by McCann–Erickson (London). How to air a politically sensitive issue without ranting and raving. This ad begs to be read.

Where would we be without the secretions of the Argentine Ant?

The search for new medicines does not, as you may suppose, always begin and end in a laboratory full of weird apparatus and white-coated boffins.

Indeed, many major discoveries have been made by apparent loonies who took it upon themselves to poke around in the most unlikely places.

And in the case of one antibacterial, this just happened to be the anal gland of the Argentine Ant (*Iridomyrmex humilis*).

A pesky little chap measuring just two millimetres, who, upon detailed examination, was found to be host to no less than 55 chemical constituents. One being the antibacterial named iridomyrmecin after its donor's Latin name. Many of the others are still the subject of minutely detailed scrutiny.

Leaving no stone unturned, in a very literal sense of the phrase, another antibacterial substance was discovered to be doing very nicely in the faeces of the blow fly larvae.

While a soil sample taken in Venezuela (where else?) was found to contain a substance which industry-based microbiologists showed to be particularly efficacious in the treatment of typhus and typhoid.

The list goes on. As does the research. But as you will by now have begun to appreciate, screening programmes involved in the search for new treatments and cures are exhaustive to say the least.

Naturally, a lot of leads may lead to nowhere. But some can provide an invaluable stepping stone to more research and occasionally to a major breakthrough itself.

One such discovery was the treatment for tuberculosis. A disease once described by Milton as the "Captain of the Men of Death." In fact, three completely different drugs were discovered, which, when used together, usually overcame any resistant strains of the disease.

And so, once further research by the pharmaceutical industry had uncovered an effective and economic means of production, the combined drugs became the standard treatment.

The impact was staggering.

Up until the 1950s, "The White Plague" had caused literally millions of deaths each year. Today, death from TB in this country is extremely rare.

All of the hospitals built for the treatment of TB have now been closed or converted. And many of the wards for infectious diseases have been given over to the care of the elderly.

Oddly enough, another drug developed from one of three tuberculosis treatments was seen to produce a marked anti-depressant effect.

After further research and development, this led to the establishment of a whole new group of medicines for the treatment of mental illness.

These, together with other recently developed psychotropic drugs, turned out to be one of the most striking examples of modern therapeutic success. Today, most of the admissions to psychiatric hospitals are shortstay patients who receive active and effective treatment.

All of this may seem a long way from the secretions of the Argentine Ant. But it is from such humble beginnings and such exhaustive research by universities, doctors, and pharmaceutical companies that these advances are made.

Advances which, in the case of TB and mental illness, have saved the health service vast sums of money by rendering hospitalisation a rarity.

In fact, it is estimated that in 1982 for example, the British Pharmaceutical Industry saved the National Health Service hospitals at least £1,658 million in England and Wales alone.

At the same time it achieved exports which, for this year, are projected to be in excess of £1,400 million.

Were it not for the funds which the pharmaceutical industry is able to reinvest in research, this healthy performance would not have been possible.

If you'd like to find out more about the British Pharmaceutical Industry, please write to: Dr. John Griffin, The ABPI, 12 Whitehall, London SW1A 2DY. **abpi**

Iridomyrmex humilis

A. Wingless Queen. Developmental Stages B. Eggs.
C. Young larva. D. Mature larvae E. Pupa.

The Association of the British Pharmaceutical Industry.

Figure 1

The first of the vaccines and the last of the Mohicans.

In the year 1800, a US presidential candidate named Thomas Jefferson explained to Chief Little Turtle and his warriors that "the Great Spirit had made a gift to the white man in showing them how to preserve themselves from the smallpox."

And so, during a visit to Washington D.C., the last of the Mohicans were duly inoculated against the disease which had been responsible for wiping out more Indian tribes than the white men themselves.

The vaccine used owed much of its origins to a Dorset farmer by the name of Benjamin Jesty. He knew of the folk belief that an attack of cowpox gave protection from smallpox and, in 1774, he saw the proof of this during a severe outbreak of the disease in his local village.

Two of his milkmaids had caught cowpox on their hands by milking cows with infected udders and had nursed their families through smallpox without catching the dreaded disease themselves.

Jesty had already had cowpox, but his wife and their two children had not. Concerned for their safety, he scratched their forearms with a 'stocking needle' based inserted the cowpox virus from the sores on the infected cows' udders. Although the Jesty family were not immune from the resulting scandal of this 'experiment', they never caught smallpox.

But the real breakthrough came some twenty years later in 1796 when Edward Jenner, an English country doctor, made the first scientific approach to the subject of immunisation.

His experiments proved the value of cowpox inoculation and the potential of artificial transmission. Not from cow to human, but from human to human, producing only a small sore at the site of inoculation and very little evidence of disease.

The now familiar name 'vaccine' was born, derived from the latin name for cowpox, 'vaccinia' (from the latin, 'vacca', a cow).

Jenner's vaccination techniques spread across the world faster than the disease itself. Napoleon had his troops vaccinated with "le vaccin jennerien" and, in honouring Jenner, was reported to have said that "he could refuse him absolutely nothing."

In Russia, the first child to be vaccinated was given the name 'Vaccinof'. Many countries made vaccination compulsory. And the newly elected President Jefferson of the USA said in a letter to Jenner, "Future nations will know by history only that the loathsome smallpox has existed and by you has been extirpated."

Prophetic words indeed. In 1980, the World Health Assembly officially declared that smallpox had been completely eradicated from the planet.

But the battle to rid the world of other diseases is still being fought. Especially in the developing countries.

The pharmaceutical industry supplies the bulk of the vaccines currently used in the World Health Organization's programme to provide immunisation for every child in the world against diphtheria, whooping cough, tetanus, measles, poliomyelitis and tuberculosis by the year 1990.

The small number of research based companies that develop and produce these vaccines are also trying to assist the less industrialised nations by producing more heat-stable products, improving distribution facilities and providing local training.

And for the future, although vaccines do not enjoy adequate patent protection, the industry is using all the recent advances in biotechnology to develop radically new immunising techniques.

Effective protection against diseases like malaria and leprosy should soon be introduced, and vaccines against other tropical diseases may well follow.

Without adequate investment, this enormous effort would not be possible.

And the people of other nations would not be so lucky as the last of the Mohicans.

If you'd like further information about the British Pharmaceutical Industry, write to: Dr. John Griffin, The ABPI, 12 Whitehall, London SW1 2DY.

The Association of the British Pharmaceutical Industry.

Figure 2

The stirrup pump, milk churn, dog bath, dairy cooler and other life saving apparatus.

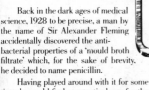

Back in the dark ages of medical science, 1928 to be precise, a man by the name of Sir Alexander Fleming accidentally discovered the anti-bacterial properties of a 'mould broth filtrate' which, for the sake of brevity, he decided to name penicillin.

Having played around with it for some time, he could find no practical use for the substance. And since it was extremely difficult to prepare sufficient amounts for experiments, he eventually discarded the stuff as a curiosity.

About ten years later, two Oxford researchers, Sir Ernst Chain and Lord Florey, decided for reasons better known to themselves to make a detailed study of moulds and bacteria. Eventually, their work led to the isolation of penicillin in a form which led to some very promising results.

And then, in 1941, the first opportunity to test the real potential of the drug presented itself in the shape of a policeman who lay critically ill with septicaemia in Oxford's Radcliffe Infirmary.

All efforts to treat him had proven useless. So in a final attempt to save his life, it was decided to use the small stock of penicillin which the two researchers had managed to produce.

His temperature dropped immediately and his condition continued to improve until the meagre supply of penicillin was used up. At which point he sadly relapsed and died. Demonstrating both the effectiveness of the drug and the difficulty of producing it in sufficient quantities.

A problem illustrated by the first 'mass production' apparatus which consisted of the rather unlikely collection of objects listed at the top of this page.

Nevertheless, enough penicillin was manufactured to achieve a series of dramatic cures, and a number of pharmaceutical companies undertook large-scale production. But hampered by the war, their techniques remained cumbersome to say the least.

One factory harvested penicillin mould from the surface of 300,000 flasks of broth, while another had over one million milk bottles in constant use.

Obviously, today's methods are rather more sophisticated. But were it not for the joint efforts of doctors, universities and pharmaceutical companies, many appalling diseases that are now easily treatable would still be taking their toll.

But there's still a long way to go.

And the British pharmaceutical industry is constantly engaged in the research and development which will hopefully provide the breakthroughs to problems like cancer, heart disease, multiple sclerosis, rheumatism, arthritis and AIDS.

You'll no doubt be aware that this kind of research requires an enormous investment of time and money.

It takes a pharmaceutical manufacturer up to 12 years to research and test a new medicine before it can be made available for doctors to prescribe. The cost of this tremendous effort can be as much as £50-£60 million for one product.

While the industry as a whole is spending over £500 million a year on research in this country.

This funding can only be generated if companies receive adequate return on sales of their existing products both at home and abroad.

We understand that these facts and figures may not be of any great revelation to you, but it's worth considering that without this kind of reinvestment, we may still have been fiddling about with stirrup pumps and dog baths.

If you'd like to find out more about the British pharmaceutical industry, please write to: Dr. John Griffin, The ABPI, 12 Whitehall, London SW1A 2DY.

The Association of the British Pharmaceutical Industry.

igure 3

Rumour has it that your confidential documents aren't!

Rumours are par for the course in business.

Most are just hearsay, but many have more than a passing relation to fact.

And those facts, as distasteful as it seems, often get passed on – in colourful black and white.

If this rings any bells, maybe you should be taking a close look at your document security.

And an even closer look at our highly efficient range of Personal paper shredders.

There are four models in the Personal shredder range, and three will sit neatly and unobtrusively beside your desk – reducing sensitive documents to unreadable shreds.

We also produce a very neat portable version that can go anywhere you go. So destruction is immediate.

Shred widths vary from 2mm to 6mm.

The choice is yours.

One final point. The sooner you find out more, the less others will be finding out about you!

Why not get in touch for the full story? We'll give you all the facts by return. Then, at least those rumours can be cut to shreds!

Name _____

Address _____

_____ Tel. No. _____

Company _____

The Breakthrough in Office Efficiency

P.O. Box 12 · Westbank · Droitwich · Worcestershire WR9 9AR
Tel 0905 776000 · Telex 338326

Figure 4

Rumour has it that your affairs are all over town.

When you're running a complex business there are certain things that should be kept strictly to yourself.

Because what other people don't know can't hurt you.

Which is good enough reason, we'd suggest, to think seriously about document security in general–and about our range of Destroyer paper shredders in particular.

The Destroyer comes in three highly efficient models.

The 2400VX, 4000 and 6000, and each is designed to shred the discarded paperwork of an entire office.

Not only that, the Destroyer 2400VX also compacts the fine particle waste making disposal no problem at all.

For the technically minded the 2400VX will accept up to 50 sheets and the 4000 will accept up to 120 sheets of A4 in one operation and shred the lot into

8mm widths. The 6000 will take a substantial 180 sheets, at a shred width of 12mm.

Why not get in touch for the full facts and figures.

Then, of course, you can have as many affairs as you like.

Name _____

Address _____

_____

Company _____

Tel. No. _____

OBM

The Breakthrough in Office Efficiency

P.O. Box 12 · Westbank · Droitwich · Worcestershire WR9 9AR
Tel 0905 776000 · Telex 338326

Figure 5

Figure 6

S THIS WHERE YOU'RE LOSING YOUR CUSTOMERS?

ost small businesses have a great
le in their operations.
's called the telephone.

nd every year it loses countless
ners and contracts.

ecause once your line is engaged,
stomer can't talk to you.

o the potential job or contract goes
here.

hat's where the new range of British
om telephone switching systems
s in.

etting you hold on to customers by
ing calls when lines are engaged,

holding calls until lines are free, informing
you through an 'alert device' that an
outside call is on the line, plus many more
features to improve business efficiency.

Ordinary telephones can't do any of
those things.

To find out more about British Telecom
switching systems and which one would
best suit your business, we need to find
out a little about yourselves.

Call us on 0272 276 646,
or complete the coupon and
return it FREEPOST today.

Then we'll get you talking.

APPROVED
for connection
to telecommunication
systems specified in the
instructions for use
subject to the
conditions set out
in them

ure 7

Figure 8

It's the traditional method of dealing with an employee with a drinking problem.

You show him the door, and close it softly behind him. Problem solved.

Why keep a bad risk on your payroll, a blot on your profit sheets, and a danger on the shop-floor?

Why tolerate a man who is too weak-willed to help himself? Anyway, since when was the treatment of alcoholics left to industry and not to statutory and voluntary agencies? Haven't we already enough problems of our own?

We understand how you feel. But we think you're wrong, for a number of reasons.

1. Not long ago, a large Glasgow firm ran a survey. They had estimated that 2 per cent of their staff would have serious drinking problems. A realistic figure, you might imagine. But they were wrong.

The real figure turned out to be between 14 and 22 per cent. Almost a quarter. And that was just at senior staff level.

We don't consider this case as anything dramatically out of the usual. For instance, if you take into account the fact that there are an estimated 60,000–80,000 alcoholics in Scotland, and that only a small percentage of this figure is receiving treatment, you can well understand the problem.

The remainder are holding down steady jobs. In commerce, and industry.

Industry, more than anyone else, has the most to lose unless alcoholics can be singled out, and given help.

What is not always realised is that lost hours, poor work, and the cost of recruiting and possibly training a new employee works out considerably more expensive than the early discovery and rehabilitation of the alcoholic.

The alcoholic is a sick man.

2. As an employer, we feel you have a responsibility towards your employees, and towards their welfare. We're sure you'll agree.

For example, we're sure you're concerned when one of your workers falls ill. Or has an accident on the shop-floor.

Why some drinkers become alcoholics and others don't is nothing to do with willpower. Or self-control.

Or strength, or weakness of character.

Alcoholism is a disease. Like arthritis, or measles.

There are particular patterns, usually starting with excessive drinking. The alcoholic may have had a problem that he found difficult to face. He turned to alcohol to bring him relief from tension and anxiety.

But all the time he underestimated the powers of alcohol as a drug. The more he drank the more tolerant he became to alcohol, and the more he had to drink to get the effect.

Now, he can't stop drinking. His mind and his body won't let him.

And because he has hangovers in the morning, and heavy drinking bouts at lunchtime, his normal work performance suffers.

He is frequently late. Some days he may not turn up at work at all. And when he does, he is in danger of causing an accident to himself and others.

Sadly, unlike any other sick person, an alcoholic may never know he is ill. He prefers to carry on and forget that he has a drinking problem.

At the one time he needs help, you give him denial.

The wrong way.

3. By handing an alcoholic his cards you do four things. First. You close your eyes to the fact that alcoholism is a disease.

Second. You ignore the fact that a member of your staff is in need of medical attention. You are as good as sacking a man with bronchitis.

Third. You palm off your problem on to some other employer. More than likely the alcoholic will find another job. His new employer will be faced with the same problems you were faced with. Chances are he'll respond in the same way.

Result. The problem is never solved, just shelved. The alcoholic is never treated at a time when there was a good chance of his rehabilitation.

Fourth. You encourage workmates to "cover-up". Because they like him, they'll carry him to avoid him being found out and fired. Feeling sorry for a sick man does not cure him. Protection and sympathy merely delay rehabilitation.

The right way.

Understand that alcoholism is an illness, and that it can be arrested.

Get this accepted by everyone concerned. Management, trade unions, employees, medical officers or company doctor, families.

In fact, make it company policy.

State clearly that:

1. An alcoholic is to be treated as a sick man, and given help.
2. The alcoholic's job is secure as long as he co-operates to the full in treatment.

This policy should be accepted as a condition of employment.

Management must understand that deciding on an actual policy is not 'do-gooding', but is in fact a financially, and economically sound proposition.

Unions should understand that the policy is concerned with a worker's welfare.

Medical Officers will be prepared to assist in making a diagnosis, arranging for treatment, and obtaining progress reports from supervisors.

Supervisors should make it their job to discourage "covering-up". They are in the best position to spot early deterioration of work performance. At the first sign of a drinking problem they can give the employee the opportunity of getting medical advice.

Action.

There's nothing experimental about deciding on a policy to deal with alcoholism in your company. You'll by no means be a pioneer.

Similar policies to the one just mentioned are already in operation. And in companies where these policies have been adopted, they're paying off. Two-thirds of the employees with drinking problems have been successfully rehabilitated.

It's a fact that a former alcoholic is very often a much harder, more conscientious worker than before he had a drinking problem.

So where do you go from here?

At this stage, just realising the size of the problem is only a start.

You're going to be saying that alcoholism is no problem in your company, partly because you'll honestly believe you don't have an alcoholic on your payroll. This could be your first mistake.

And when you discover an employee with a drinking problem your second mistake could be how you decide to treat him.

A long term policy of rehabilitation may not be as easy as a policy of dismissal. But we think with a short term solution you lose in the long run.

And not just you, industry as a whole can ill afford to lose in times like these.

Write for our leaflet "The Employed Problem Drinker" to this address:
The Scottish Health Education Unit,
Freepost, Edinburgh, EH12 0PQ.

"We know how to treat alcoholics in our company. We fire them."

Figure 9

Figure

For a little more than a pound we'll get rid of your nagging wife.

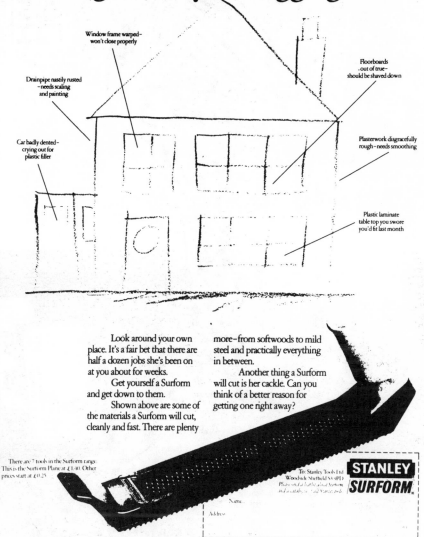

Window frame warped – won't close properly

Drainpipe nastily rusted – needs scaling and painting

Car badly dented – crying out for plastic filler

Floorboards out of true – should be shaved down

Plasterwork disgracefully rough – needs smoothing

Plastic laminate table top you swore you'd fit last month

Look around your own place. It's a fair bet that there are half a dozen jobs she's been on at you about for weeks.

Get yourself a Surform and get down to them.

Shown above are some of the materials a Surform will cut, cleanly and fast. There are plenty more – from softwoods to mild steel and practically everything in between.

Another thing a Surform will cut is her cackle. Can you think of a better reason for getting one right away?

There are 7 tools in the Surform range. This is the Surform Plane at £1.40. Other prices start at £0.25

To: Stanley Tools Ltd
Woodside Sheffield S3 9PD
Please send a leaflet about Surform and availability of Surform tools.

Name

Address

STANLEY
SURFORM

Figure 11

Why my father is a beast

"Actuarially speaking," I remarked to my father, "you are close to being
no longer here. I am enquiring, therefore, whether the provision
you have made for the family well-being has kept pace with the
inflationary trends which we all deplore.
The beast said nothing. Just reached in his desk and thumped me
on the ear with a life insurance policy. I must say, it *felt* big enough!"

Figure 12

DIFFICULT CHOICE ISN'T IT?

What will it be like to travel to France by the Channel Tunnel?

Take a deep breath before you begin your journey. It may be the last fresh air you enjoy until you reach France. It seems certain that the Channel Tunnel will not match the fume-free atmosphere legally demanded on board car ferries.

The problem of inadequate ventilation becomes more alarming when you consider the real possibilities of being trapped in the Channel Tunnel.

Trapped in a hold-up caused by breakdowns, traffic jams or, even worse, an accident. If you suffer from claustrophobia, it doesn't bear thinking about.

Artificial lighting is another gloomy prospect. It's generally accepted that this contributes significantly to driver fatigue.

Allied to these environmental concerns, are the questions of journey time and cost.

There is little evidence to suggest that the Channel Tunnel will be quicker than the ferry routes. Or cheaper.

In contrast, consider a trip by ferry.

You can stroll on the deck, enjoy the view, breathe in the sea air. Or, simply relax in a comfortable lounge.

Enjoy a meal in the restaurant. Browse in the shops. Pick-up your foreign currency at the exchange bureau.

And, of course, take advantage of the duty-free facilities. (How do you buy duty-free goods in a tunnel?)

It's up to you to choose which way you cross the Channel. But if the Channel Tunnel forces the ferries out of business, you'll have no choice to make.

THE CHANNEL TUNNEL
The black hole that will put Britain in the red.

Flexilink

CAMPAIGN FOR ROYAL CHANNEL FERRIES

gure 13

9   Words, campaigns, research and things

It happens from time to time that aspiring copywriters turn up at my office and harass me into giving them a job or, at least, talk me into helping them get one elsewhere. The bigger specimens of these – those I can't throw out – usually get their own way. One enterprising young chap turned up every day for a week half-an-hour before I did, and I would find him at my desk working away like mad. His tenacity appealed, so I took him on for a year. He's now working for a ten million pound agency – and doing very nicely thank you.

It comes to pass, when I find it in my heart to waste time, energy and money on someone who will forget I even exist the moment he gets himself gainfully employed, that I sit the newcomer down to see what he, or she, can do. I wait with baited breath, because I know that as surely as night follows day, the first of our tyro's headline submissions will contain certain classic faults. These defects show up time after time, that is until my exasperation finally imposes itself and they desist. The transgressions are the use of words and phrases – particular words and phrases – which to my mind no longer have any more substance than a puff of wind.

I propose, first, to take the word quality.

Quality is a very fine thing. It is, I should say, the one

attribute that every manufacturer wishes to claim for his product. This is good. This is praiseworthy. This is natural. But it is a word you would be well advised never to use during your copywriting career; and, come 2030, you may be pleasantly surprised to find how well you've got on without it. Quality is, without doubt, the most abused word in the whole of advertising. It has been put through the mangle so often that it has been wrung dry of its last meaning or significance. Used on its own, as it usually is, it has no more corporeal being than Marley's ghost.

Naturally, every manufactured item has some aspect of quality about it – or some qualities that distinguish it from the competition. If it hasn't, why is it being made? And, of course, it is sensible and rational to talk about this quality or these qualities in the advertising. But, please, by all that's reasonable *specifically* and not generally.

Too many companies, when asked by an enquiring customer or an eager-beaver agency to put their finger on their main sales point, proudly declaim. 'Why – can't you see – it's quality.' Ask them precisely what they mean and they are floundering around looking for superlatives.

Advertising has moved a long way since the days when it was enough to claim that one's product was 'best'. But advertising has not yet moved far enough from the insipid claim of quality. These days, quality is as empty of meaning, when unsupported, as by now those sparkling bottles you got last Christmas are empty of drink. Be specific, I have said. To this I would add: wherever you can, be factual. Consumer advertising may be able to afford to sell dreams-come-true, hopes realized and ambitions fulfilled. But the other kind, the industrial – upon which you will almost certainly be labouring eighty per cent of your time – operates in a harsher climate.

Facts are the order of the day. By facts I mean facts and not windy claims. It is not sufficient simply to shout that a product does a job quicker, or easier or cheaper. How much quicker? How much easier? How much cheaper? And why? And if you can support the 'how' with proof, so much the better. So *very* much the better.

Other words in this category – meaning that they have no meaning in the context of which they are used – are 'value', 'reliability' and good old 'expertise'. Stay away from them. Better by far to write an ad that says you can run your central heating for the cost of a pint of beer per day than say it 'offers value for money'. More impressive by miles is the proposition that a customer has owned a particular vacuum-cleaner for fifteen years than tell people that 'this vacuum-cleaner is reliable'. Believable is the announcement that all so-and-so's mechanics have been 'trained by Mercedes' rather than say they have technical expertise.

I do go on, don't I? Damn good job I do, otherwise quite a few people would be running around this and other countries digging up roads for a living!

We come to phrases.

I saw an ad the other day for a brassiere manufacturer who, for the sake of public decency shall remain nameless. The product, you will be entranced to learn, comes in a *free* presentation envelope. I am not, however, picking on the abuse of the word 'free', although I could if I felt in the mood. It's almost like John Player offering Superking fags in a free black-and-gold packet. No, there's worse. The bit about the ad which caused me to gnash my teeth was the headline '*Made lovingly – especially for you*'. Now these bra's cost about six quid and are available from countless branches of a well-known chain store, not to mention elsewhere. So, any Janet or Jane doesn't have to look too far in order to get the appropriate, up-lift, cross-stretch, separation and whatever else this bra offers. They must be sold in the hundreds of thousands, if not the millions.

How, then, can anyone muster sufficient gall to look the women of this country in the corporate bust and declare to each and every one of them that these bras are 'especially for her'?

Not that I expect anyone to take up arms about it. But if you maltreat words in this fashion they wither and die. Those I've mentioned above have been done to death and in their murder, have dragged some of the standing of advertising into the grave with them.

* * *

I now propose to change the subject, but not completely.

Apart from being infatuated with advertising (albeit, as usual, a one-sided affair), I am also hopelessly in love with words. Thus, I like words to say what they mean; or alternatively to mean what they say. Forgive me, therefore, if I take up a little of your time to protest against the practically universal misuse of the word 'campaign'.

A series of ads about the same product, with unrelated headlines, unrelated pictures and unrelated copy are . . . a series of ads. Whatever else they may be, a campaign is most certainly and very definitely what they aren't.

Let's get our drinks straight. A campaign is a series of ads in which the same basic thought, or the same basic sales strategy is expressed in terms of variations on a theme. The essence of a campaign is that it should have some intrinsic continuity – of design, of typography, of format, of the tone of the copy, or of all the lot. A collection of unrelated ads, no matter how good they may be individually, does not add up to a campaign; because the principle of a campaign is that each part of it, by its obvious resemblance to all the other parts, gains added recognition and added strength. The whole, to coin a phrase, becomes greater than the sum of its parts. That's the theory, anyhow.

Now I am by no means putting it forward as a cast-iron rule that all campaigns should be *campaigns* – if you see what I mean. Some of the best ads are one-offs, and I should be the last to advocate not using them simply because they can't be extended into a series. However, to bash the point home, a campaign should be *seen* to be a campaign. It should be a natural campaign, rather than a theme that has been squeezed, until its eyes watered, in an effort to milk the idea over the looked-for number of ads.

Most agency personnel, and indeed most advertisers, when considering any kind of planned advertising, think automatically of around six or more ads, all patently having the same mother and father. Any ideas, however bright, which don't conform to the pattern tend to be rejected as evincing distressing signs of illegitimacy. This, at its face value, is a perfectly reasonable attitude. It is one that has been adopted since time immemorial; and fifty million advertisers can't be wrong. What I would say, though – and what I am going to say – is that it suffers from three fundamental weaknesses; there are probably more, but three will do to be going on with.

First, it rests on the assumption that the people whom you wish to impress with the repetition-value of a series will see all of the ads in that series, or at least most of them; and that they have both the wit and the interest to recognize the family connection as between one ad and another. In most cases, this is a dreadfully optimistic assumption.

Second, when a copywriter or a designer (or, in extreme cases, an executive) has a sound idea for an ad, it is liable to be bent and distorted until it screams for mercy, as I've implied, in order to string it out over an unnatural number of permutations. This frequently happens. In fact, now that I come to think of it deeply, it practically *always* happens. And, of course, it's bad news – because the longer a series goes on, the weaker it becomes.

Third, when a good idea comes along that patently can't be expanded into a series, the chances are that it will never see the light of day; never be allowed out of the agency's front door. I weep to think of all the brightness and ingenuity which has been stifled on these grounds.

Rule 9   *Nobody should be anti-series for the sake of it; but everybody should reserve the right to be anti-pro-series.*

I will concede that it is possible for a series of ads to be so radically different, each from the other, that this very difference can, paradoxically, add up to a sort of inverted family feeling. But to pursue this thought would be to wander into the fields of the metaphysical; and, here, we are concerned only with simply generalities – us being simple souls.

If you were to spend as much time looking at industrial media as I do (and I wouldn't wish it on a dog), you may be struck, as I have been, by the marked absence of recognizable campaigns as opposed to just ads. This I feel reflects on agencies in general, and company ad-managers in particular. It implies that they don't sit down calmly together, every so whenever, to plan both their advertising strategy and the tactics which will enable them to win their strategic ends. It suggests that too many ads are prepared on an *ad hoc* basis – often with overlooked copy-dates breathing down their necks. This may be a ghastly libel; it is also a ghastly truth.

Anyone who has ever worked within fifteen miles of an agency knows what the result of such off-the-cuff operating is likely to be. Campaigns are prepared by copywriter/ designer teams; for good or ill, they have a certain stamp put on them. One-off ads, especially urgent one-off ads, are likely to be handed out to whichever writer or designer happens to be free at the time. And writers and designers being the contrary and mercenary lot they are, it's six-to-four on that the last thing they will do, unless forced into it with threats of confiscation of the key to the drinks cupboard, is to follow a style set by someone else. In that way is the confusion compounded; thus is identity dissipated, hence comes the patchwork quiltery of so many so-called campaigns.

It doesn't make for good advertising; it doesn't make for good relations between agency and client; and it has the net result – if you're the copywriter lumbered with this sort of work – of giving you a personal portfolio of ads which leave the impression of someone leaping about like a demented grasshopper.

Enough.

* * *

I said earlier that we'd have a word or two on the subject of research. Perhaps the best course to take, here, is one that gives an actual instance of research in action – then you can make up your own mind.

Every so often an agency is asked to produce advertising material for an account which is, in every respect, totally different from the straightforward, informative type stuff the account has been used to. This usually happens, as it happened in the example I will quote, when a new advertising manager heaves on to the client scene. This particular chap was all bright eye and bushytail; and his given reason for changing from the competent, hard-working ads we'd been putting together, to a series of off-beat productions which neither showed the product nor talked about products except in a very general way, was to gauge the response via research. With this research, he told us, he would be better able to plan ongoing advertising. He would also be researching the earlier work, of course. Given this as a brief, the agency launched itself full-tilt into the job required. We were delighted to be able to show how way out we could be.

Well, the off-beat material fared badly. In fact, the ordinary ads out-pulled it in reader noting, memorability, etc. by more than ten times.

A chastening experience, I can tell you. We argued, you won't be surprised to learn, that the new ads hadn't been given sufficient opportunity to prove themselves. But it failed to wash. Back we went to the old style – and I'm afraid with much more old and a good deal less style.

Something about this whole business made me slightly uneasy, and since the same thing continues to happen today in agencies up and down the country, I remain uneasy. For that reason, I propose to utter one or two generalities.

One swallow doesn't make a pub-crawl. One chapter doesn't make a Ku-Klux Klan. Nor does one book of research documents make a bible. Speaking for myself, I might well take such evaluations as we've been talking about as a *pointer*. I would certainly not take them as having the same divine authority as Moses' tablets.

If advertising could be dragooned, drilled and rationalized and made to work in accordance with a set of rules, life would be a fair bit easier for a lot of us. But it can't. Any attempt to make it behave as if it were an exact science is destined to end in egregious failure.

The possible permutations of any given advertising situation are as numerous as the possible permutations of having-it-off on the pools. Within very broad limits, research can tell you (or indicate to you) whether or not the ad you chose to run worked. What it can't tell you is whether the next one you choose *will* work. Those techniques which set out to forecast in advance the likely success or failure of any advertising (concept-testing, pre-publication copy testing, and so on), I view with the deepest distrust. Having attended some of these sessions – where members of the public are asked, in exchange for cash, to give their opinions, in a wide range of respects, on proposed ads – I have very good reason to be doubtful.

Advertising, thank the Lord, is still very much a matter of doing what your bones tell you to be right – and any copywriter who doesn't view it that way should see an osteopath.

There you are, I said I'd let you make your own mind up – didn't I? But wait. For an even more ludicrous example of research, please turn to Chapter 11 and see under the heading: Research isn't definitive.

* * *

To round off this chapter, let me point you in the general direction of a thing called the Trades Descriptions Act. This piece of legislation hit the statute book in 1968; and while there have been several amendments to it – plus the setting up of various watchdog bodies – the original proposition remains largely the same, that, in my words, it is an indictable offence punishable by up to two years' imprisonment, for a trader to make an untrue statement or a false claim about a product or service. I have not, I must confess, read every word of the act, but I am aware that an advertising agency is a trader's agent, a trader's aider and abetter; and, as such, I would guess just as likely to wind up serving two years in prison as the trader himself in the event of contravening the act.

The legislation is intended to inhibit liars, crooks, gold brick merchants, green-goods men and outright sharks. But, like many another piece of legislation before it, in flinging out a net to catch sharks, it ends up hauling in schools of innocent minnows.

The verbal or written expression of a perfectly proper enthusiasm about a product or service, which is part and parcel of any selling operation (and that includes copywriting), is likely to land someone on the inside looking out. It isn't exactly as bad as that, but if you know what's good for you, you'll refrain from knowingly and deliberately perpetrating untruths.

I'll agree that very few whoppers are to be found in advertising these days. Though there are any number of minor fabrications which, on analysis, can be put down to over-optimism about a product on the part of the client, along with full-supporting naivety on the part of the writer.

You have surely seen those ads for do-it-yourself green-houses or garden sheds. 'Can be erected by a man and a boy in three hours', they assert confidently. And so they can. But it becomes apparent, in the ensuing struggle to build this thing, that the man and the boy to whom they so glibly refer should be none other than Sir Robert McAlpine and Son.

So beware of the bull.

Rule 10 *A transparent lie will collapse under scrutiny. The truth won't. You don't need legislation to prove the wisdom of that.*

Summary

1   Some words ain't what they used to be; and some words aren't anything at all now, employed as they have been over the years as a substitute for hard facts.

Take this little gem, lifted from ad copy in a women's magazine:

> *It (the product) has everything that is attractive in modern styling, not to mention our assurance of unsurpassed quality allied to excellent workmanship. . . .*

What does it all mean? Who, I would ask, is the arbiter of what's attractive in modern styling? Furthermore, on the off-chance that I find *anything* redeemable in modern styling, do they know what it is? Of course they don't. And there's that confounded word 'quality' again, with only that other confounded word 'surpassed' to back it up.

It's empty; it's passionless; it's meaningless. Now it doesn't matter much whether the ad in which this line made its ghastly appearance was trying to promote electric egg-timers or a range of plastic macs – nor whether the rest of the ad was above reproach, which it wasn't. The point is that the line was thrown in as the written equivalent of elevator muzak, to pad out the distance between start and finish. At least, that's what I think was meant. It surely wasn't designed to be a serious contribution? Was it?

Apart from those already given in the text, two more words well-worth avoiding are 'ideal' and 'invaluable' – especially when used, as they almost always are, to loosely establish a use for a product. In which case, you get: 'Invaluable to motorists' and 'Ideal for the man who has everything'. The way I see it, there's only one gadget that could truly be called ideal for the man who has everything. And that's a burglar alarm.

2 Fight the attractiveness of using devious purple prose when a straightforward, black-and-white statement of fact would do the job more effectively, more believably.

Advertising for products aimed at women appears to be the most culpable in this regard. I read statements such as: 'Lovingly prepared for the essential you', from a cosmetics house and immediately conjure up visions of hundreds of workers on a production-line, hand in loving hand, or hand in loving blouse/trouser if you like, as they slop great mounds of cream into endless lines of jars.

I ask you?

3 Truth is a delicate flower, yet some advertisers handle it with all the care they'd bring to a coal-hammer.

I, and I expect you also, receive mailing shots telling me that I have been singled out from millions to take part in a national competition, or that I have won stage-one of a competition which, if I care to enter for stage-two, could win me a new car, or a set of matching jug-handles, or even both.

Great – except I know that every householder in the neighbourhood has been mailed likewise.

I am sure that the uptake on these promotions is very

high and the promotions houses responsible very rich –
but is this gambit strictly honest? In order to be sure, I'd
one day have to receive from them a mailer saying:

*Sorry, mate, the computer figures you are a non-starter. You blew
it.*

Not much chance of that, methinks.

10 Radio and television –
the bare facts

Everything I've said about press copy, generally speaking, applies equally to radio and television commercial scripting. Your spot must be attractively presented and contain information useful to the recipient. Over and above that, there are no limits to the verbal and visual opportunities offered by these media.

Of the two, radio is the closest to my heart. I happen to think that, unlike television, it forces the listener to use his imagination – his visual imagination. Television presents sounds and images that are hard and fast. There is nothing more to be gained from it, or read into it. Radio, on the other hand, leaves room for listener interpretation; and in the so doing gets the audience working on its behalf.

It's only my opinionated preference, of course, and one that you may not go right along with; and I for one wouldn't blame you. But I don't think it would be wise for anybody to underestimate its power.

I have no intention of discussing radio and television production techniques, here. The subject is too vast to be covered in just a few pages – always supposing I know enough about it, anyway. What I will say is that, compliments of the microchip, anything is possible.

Anything that can be dreamed up can also be translated into sound or film, either by expert editing, by talented camera work, or by computer-programmed trickery. New video techniques take most of the pain and a lot of the expense out of special effects work. Where standard 35 mm film might spend days in a laboratory having a special effect processed and patched into the main body of the film, an identical 'optical' may be obtained in minutes on a video desk. Squeeze zooms, match-dissolves, spins, revolves, tumbles, wipes and superimpositions are much easier to achieve with video techniques. A good argument can be made, though, for greater flexibility – especially for location work – and a higher quality of reproduction with film; but since all film is transferred to tape for transmission in any case, I'll leave the technical discussion to someone more qualified.

*   *   *

The simplest method I can think of for getting to grips with radio and television scripting is to work through a hypothetical brief, establishing each basic element as we go. Also, I think it wiser to begin with radio. We shall, therefore, suppose that the client is a national chain of men's tailoring shops and a forty-second spot is what's called for.

I am tempted to christen this firm with the name Next On Top Is Austin; and on account of I can resist anything except temptation, I will.

With forty seconds in which to say something profound – we'll find out what, exactly, in a moment – let us, for now, examine in detail the length of time available and come to a conclusion about it from the writer's point of view.

In an ideal world, we would now be dashing off a swift memo cordially inviting the media person responsible for allocating those forty seconds to go and boil his head. In an ideal world, you see, the script would be written as if time was no object; and when we were happy with it, we'd time it.

And that's the length the commercial would be. But in this far from ideal world, we'd never get away with it. Apart from falling out with the media person, who would need to re-hash his schedules, I'd hate to be the one to present the client with a bill for a series of twenty-five-minute radio commercials.

Which means we are lumbered with forty seconds; which also means that the piece must be accurately timed and, if anything, should run slightly under.

When timing a script, take into account every syllable of dialogue, every note of music, every door-closing, bell-ringing, car-starting, foot-stepping item of sound-effect and, just as importantly, every pause separating these items. And it's as well to remember that pauses have both a dimension in time and an auditory value. Where would comedians be without pauses? Out-of-work comedians, no question. On no account attempt to fill all the legitimate gaps; in no way endeavour to fill the commercial with forty second's worth of distance run. Pace it naturally.

Writers of commercials which hurl loud and rapid words at their listeners need not be amazed at an indifferent response. They built the disinterest into the piece themselves simply by presuming that the audience would take the trouble to decipher the dialogue. It never does and it very certainly never will.

As with press ads, the softer the word and the more intriguing the proposition, the better the reaction. To my way of thinking, this holds just as true with television work.

Each of us has seen, day after infuriating day, certain TV spots which, by their sheer banality of content, leave us feeling that suicide might not be such a bad idea after all. They talk to us as if they were playing to a convention of village idiots; and the offending pieces always include an infinitely repeatable phrase or 'hit-line' such as: 'If the pans won't scour, you've got to have power. Apollo does the job'. This is reiterated ad nauseam throughout the commercial to such effect that one is begging for the swift release of a bullet in the head.

Unarguably, someone, somewhere, is convinced that an approach of this kind has its benefits; and it could be argued that, in one respect at least, he is correct – since if you repeat something often enough and loud enough, sooner or later its content will be absorbed. (A long succession of dictators has grasped this simple principle in the cradle.) Though whether the message will be believed for its own sake, or for the reason that the listener is too punch-drunk to care why he believes it, is another matter entirely.

I suspect that the originators of such material are singularly unmindful either way. But I reserve the right to suggest that a subtler approach would win more friends and influence more people than does the Mao's-little-red-book formula.

Another aspect of the genre I'm talking about is the downright unbelievability of the situations and dialogue we are asked to accept:

'Oh, Melanie, you're not still using those old- fashioned pan scourers?' The question is posed, not without a touch of patronizing contumely, by housewife 1. This lady is dressed as though she has just stepped from Liberty's window. All the while, housewife 2, who is an obvious twerp, who clearly shouldn't be allowed near anything as complicated as a pan, and who has Oxfam for a tailor, looks suitably cowed. 'Yes,' she confides, 'And all my pans are so badly scratched, too.'

It is a matter of great wonder to me how two women of such colossally different tastes and intellects can even speak to each other, never mind trade handy hints about pan cleaning. I mention it only as a passing observation.

Meanwhile, back at the commercial:

'But what can I do about it?' asks number 2. 'Nothing will get *these* clean.'

'That's where you're wrong,' says number 1 with school-girl cockiness. 'It's simple.' It's *always* simple. 'Try Apollo on all your non-stick pots and pans. It brings them up as good as new.' At which point, she produces from somewhere about her person a tub/bottle/tube of the product – mandatorily shaped like a phallus – and nuzzles it close to her face. She trots out the spiel: 'If the pans won't scour . . .' and so on.

In my own minor experiment with life, I have found that people do not normally interlocute in this product-benefit orientated kind of way. I know it; you know it. Presumably, then, the writers and directors of such films also know it. I'll say nothing about the actresses, who must surely be opiated by the gross crassness of it all. For goodness sake, even the assistant to the studio's third electrician, as unworldly as he may be, knows it.

Anyway, returning to the commercial, we have cut to 'later' and our two chums are helping out at the Girl Guides' bunfight in the local drill-hall. Oxfam, it seems, has been out touting in some salubrious neighbourhoods, because woman number 2 is now wearing an expensive little number from St Laurent – so she is on a sartorial par with number 1.

Number 1: 'So glad you could find time to help out today, Melanie.'

Number 2: 'Well, I soon had those pans done – thanks to Apollo.' With which she conjures a saucepan from the folds of her frock and demonstrates its pristine non-scratchedness to the camera. Followed by: 'If the pans won't scour . . .' You know the rest.

How any woman could believe a single word of it sufficiently to go out and buy the product defies understand-ing. I beg of you, from the bottom of my heart, never to be responsible for material of this abysmal like. It is beyond defence.

Then why do they do it? Ah, now you're asking. I believe they do it because their research tells them to do it – or, rather, because their interpretation of the research tells them to do it. There can be no other sane reason, or indeed, insane reason, depending on which way your mind works.

* * *

My apologies for going off at a tangent, but it needed saying. Mayhap we should return to the radio spot and discuss the brief in full.

We learn that Next On Top Is Austin is an old-established, high-street outfitters. Until recently, their image was 'gents natty three-piece suit' of the bespoke kind, retailed from shops that bore a perceivable resemblance to Victorian museums. The market was in the upper age-range; but it seems that the thirties to sixties males were buying fewer suits, going instead for casual slacks, sports jackets and blousons. In an attempt to halt the decline, the firm changed its name from Colliburts, changed its corporate image, changed the look of its shops, and changed its stock to include a wide range of the clothes mentioned above.

In consequence, the company picked up a younger market and profits rose. Yet Next On Top Is Austin continues to be a traditional tailor for all that; and it wishes to retain its reputation for producing first-class made-to-measure suits. After all, the company's tailoring skills are such that it can make suits which hide paunches, disguise dropping shoulders, conceal silly walks, and generally mask from public view the physical practical-jokes which nature has played on most of us.

Any promotional venture, therefore, should stress this accomplishment. Furthermore, it should stress it to the twenties to thirties market – prospective executives, bride-grooms, bright job-hunters – as well as the traditional purchaser. It will also suggest that with modern materials and fashionable colours, the suit-wearer need not look like a professional pall-bearer.

That's the brief and our task is to fulfil it with an attention-getting commercial. Initially, we need a concept; one that will appeal to both ends of the audience spectrum. Well, I guess we could plump for a bland, inoffensive platform of authoritative voice-over which delivers the message straightforwardly: 'Whatever the fashion trend, people still like to see you in a well-cut nicely-styled suit. In fact, most business organizations demand it. . . .'

Contrariwise, we might do the identical job by writing a jingle along the lines of:

> *When you're going to the altar, or looking for a job,*
> *Or making business calls around the town*
> *In a suit you'll look far better, than you would in slacks and sweater,*
> *And your name will then be known with some renown.*

Don't laugh – you would be most surprised to see what a talented jingle-composer can do with banalities such as this. To confirm it, take some time to listen to a few random jingles currently running, then write them out and read them, so to speak, in cold blood. Not so amusing, but certainly as interesting, is the knowledge that the best of the jingle-houses charge anything from £2000 to £30,000, or more, for an original composition – based, of course, on the writer's words.

But I like neither of those approaches, anyway. Both tend to favour the younger market too strongly. Can't we dream up a pitch that satisfies the oldsters, too?

'Where do you get your ideas from?' The question is unavoidable when in non-advertising circles; it's also wholly unanswerable wherever you happen to be. If I knew from whence, I'd patent it pretty smartly. Ideas just happen. One minute you're staring at a blank sheet of paper in the typewriter, making anagrams of Olivetti, and the next – wallop! – it's salvation come to call. Very often, though, inspiration comes from others, right out of the blue. The trick is to recognize it when it happens.

By way of explanation, and so as to craftily introduce the solution to the problem now before us, permit me to quote part of a conversation I was involved in not many days ago. It happened at a pilots' meeting in the bar of the flying club. A fellow aviator was holding forth about the annual medicals we are obliged to undergo.

'Did you know,' he asked, 'that three per cent of all trainee pilots are found to be colour-blind?'

To which another of the company replied: 'And the rest of us just dress that way.'

It brought the house down; and not only because we were collectively up to here in a variety of well-known beverages. It was a good line – maybe not an original line, but right up our street. So much so, with a slight adjustment, it's a gift for Next On Top Is Austin.

But, first, what of the treatment? Shall we go for a plain, unvarnished voice-over? A conversational piece? Or a not-so-straight voice-over using a well-known personality?

An investigation is in order.

1 We can reject the announcement-type voice-over unless, of course, we are prepared to use the line as a statement of fact; and I don't think such forthrightness as I have in mind would be a good bet in these circumstances. We might, quite reasonably, consider a single voice where the voice itself contains a hint of the comic. I'm talking of a strong regional accent (different from the region we are broadcasting to, certainly), or a foreign accent, or a nasal/adenoidal delivery.

2 Any personality we employed in this context would obviously be a comedian or some kind of humorous commentator. I'd go along with that but for one small consideration. We should be obliged to find a personality who would feel happy about delivering the line. To put it another way, the syntactical differences in writing for, say,

Terry Wogan as compared with Terry Scott are chalk and cheese. When you're working with big names, it's important to study their particular brand of humour. That goes without saying. Just as critical is an intimacy with their pace, timing and idiosyncratic usage of key words – quite apart from catch-phrases, chuckles, sniffs and sighs.

Some while ago, I put together a radio script for the London Dungeon which featured the superb voice of Vincent Price. I was surprised, but extremely gratified, when he changed not a single word. He was comfortable with my script, and I was overjoyed with the fact of that. It won't surprise you that I spent many hours perfecting the script – writing and re-writing to a mental sound-picture of the actor. For his part, the recording was in the can within an hour. I believe they call it professionalism.

At any rate, selecting a personality specifically for this exercise is obviously out of the question. What's more, whoever we choose might well trump us with an invoice.

What I can do, though, purely for demonstration's sake, is reproduce a thirty-second radio script I wrote for the London Dungeon featuring the inimitable and much-missed Leonard Rossiter. If you are unfamiliar with the London Dungeon, it's a quite unique waxworks which majors on British mediaeval history – with all the gory bits left in. Its location, in dank vaults beneath London Bridge, adds to the horror of it all.

Here's the script:

> *SFX (sound effects): telephone answer-pips, plus coin dropping into coin-box. Slight echo on voice*

VO: Leonard Rossiter (From his point-of-view, with fast, anxious delivery):

> 'Hello, hello . . . is that the manager of the London Dungeon . . . the only exhibition of British mediaeval history in the world?
>
> Yes, well, I've got a complaint.

What, what – me squeamish? Huh. Seeing all
those tortures and Anne Boleyn getting her head
chopped off doesn't bother me.

Oh, dear, no – a skeleton hanging on a gibbet
doesn't worry me.

I've seen more blood at one of Miss Whatser-
name's coffee mornings.

Eh? Well, yes, of course I've been there. It's
under London Bridge, and you're open seven days.

But that . . . er . . . that's the problem, see. I'm *at*
the London Dungeon now . . .

Er . . . locked in . . .'

SFX: hollow footsteps approaching the mike

'And . . . it's . . . er . . . getting . . . pretty . . . dark.'

(Fade on footsteps.)

For the full effect it would be necessary to hear the finished
recording. But it may help if you can recall Leonard
Rossiter's masterful performances as the seedy landlord in
that hilarious television series. His rapid, nervous delivery,
along with his ability to project bravado liberally laced with
cowardice, are the foundations of the script. In particular,
the 'locked-in' phrase is so cleverly understated that I hold
this piece of work among my all-time favourites.

You may have discerned a marked lack of 'sell' in the
script. So have others. Then perhaps I should disclose that,
all things having been made equal, this radio spot brought
visitors to the London Dungeon in greater numbers than any
commercial before it. How they evaluated such response
remains a mystery to me. All I know is what I was told; and
believe me, accolades from clients are so few and far between
in this business that one is unlikely to forget them, or confuse
them with something else. 'Sell', therefore, can be just as
powerful when it's implied as when it's expressed.

Anyway, all this has nothing whatsoever to do with Next On Top Is Austin – so let's get back to it.

*   *   *

3 We now arrive at conversational, or dialogue treatments. Given forty seconds in which to present a sales message via a two-way dialogue, and we have all the ingredients for disaster. If you have ever taped a real-life conversation, you will know that the pauses, throat-clearings and stutters often occupy more tape-time than the words. Relate that to radio dialogue and the absurdity dawns. What sounds natural is grossly unnatural, and vice versa. Add to that the reason for the whole charade – the sales pitch – and the magic can very soon drift out of a copywriter's life.

Very well. We've explored all the nooks and crannies. Where are we? Stuck with a half-dialogue, half-voice-over script, is where we are. Shall we proceed?

Imagine, if you will, a flashy and less-than-illustrious gent's outfitter. His shop in the high street is all tinted mirror and shoddy clothes. The greater part of his off-the-peg stock of trendy fashions and traditional (sic) suits is mass pro-duced in the Far East – and any guarantee he may give, runs out the minute you reach the pavement. The scenario, then, is this:

> *Interior of dodgy gent's outfitters. We use a male assistant (MA) and an authoritative male voice over (MVO) chipping-in as we progress.*
>
> *SFX: shopping crowd effects and mood music a la muzak*

MA: Male assistant (Cockney wide-boy delivery):
'Ow, that looks a *treat*, sir. Here, just look in the mirror – a perfect suit, if I may say so.

What? Sleeves too long? Ah, well, it's your arms, mate.

They're a bit on the short side.

But they will wear in. . . .'

(Fade and up-fade male voice over.)

MVO: 'Whatever the fashion trend, there's always a time when you need a well-cut, professionally tailored suit.

And at Next On Top Is Austin that's exactly what you get. Plus the widest possible choice of styles, materials and colours . . . And no flannel – unless you specifically request it.'

(Fade and up-fade male assistant et al.)

MA: 'Ow, very smart, guv'nor. Pea-green with maroon stripes – what can I *say*?

A yellow shirt to set it off, perhaps . . .?'

(Fade and up-fade MVO.)

MVO: 'Next On Top Is Austin. Like we say: three per cent of the population is colour-blind. The rest just dress that way.'

Maybe – maybe not. But something in that area should do the trick. Were you to push me into a corner (though to do that, you'd need to be female and not all that fussy about whom you push into corners), I'd say that it doesn't hit the market quite as well as it ought. Might I then be so bold as to suggest that you work it up until it does?

What we ought to do now is examine a few random, and deliberately condensed, briefs to see if our earlier thoughts about treatment are as sensible as they appeared when I wrote them. We (and that means you) should also be able to pick up a trick or two on how to distil a broad concept into a small, but heady little number; and how to be pithy without sounding awkward or wooden.

The first, a forty-second spot, is on behalf of a world-famous hand-tool manufacturer. It's Leystan Tools, no less.

This company manufactures the definitive range of excellently engineered tools. Saws, chisels, planes – you name it. The object of our exercise is to reinforce in the minds of the tool-buying public the notion that under the Leystan Tools banner, they will find just about every type of hand-tool that was ever invented. In particular, the company wishes to push its hammer range – which is comprehensive. Claw hammers; pin-hammers; ball-pein hammers; and Steelshaft hammers.

So we now have a list of products: a long list of products. Can you, therefore, see any good reason why we shouldn't present the list – or as much of it as time allows – as the substance of the commercial? Neither can I.

I propose that we do it, with a single voice, in this way:

Male voice over has a cultivated, somewhat over-the-top accent; and he employs a clipped, precise delivery – rather like an army general briefing the troops. As the script progresses, however, he becomes increasingly unnerved, finally to regain his composure.

> *SFX: Various hammering sequences throughout.*

MVO: (Clears throat)
'Hm-hum . . . Right, now. Leystan, as you all should know, make hand-tools.
Leystan make saws, chisels, planes and rules . . .'

> *SFX: Light hammering*

MVO: 'And . . they . . . make . . . pin . . . hammers.
As I was saying, Leystan make hand-drills, breast-drills and push-drills . . .'

> *SFX: Hammering on softwood (louder)*

MVO: 'And, indeed, yes, they make claw hammers.
Leystan make screwdrivers, vices, marking tools and knives . . .'

> *SFX: Hammering on hardwood (louder still)*

MVO: 'And they make Steelshaft hammers – for crying out loud!
    Um . . . fine . . . Leystan make jack-planes, block-planes and bench planes . . .'

SFX: Hammering on sheet metal (much louder)

MVO: (Shouts) 'And . . . they . . . make . . . ball-pein . . . hammers!'

SFX: Hammering stops abruptly on 'ball-pein'

MVO: (Caught in mid-shout) 'Er, hammers. And what's more, Leystan hand-tools make light work of heavy going.
    Any questions so far? OK.
    Now, Leystan make spokeshaves, try-squares, levels, pliers, mitre-boxes . . .'
(Fade to time)

Script exercise

It so happens that the above, as you have not failed to notice, is a play on the ubiquitous Stanley Tools name – though the script is wholly fabricated. By happy coincidence, it also happens that I perform occasional chores for this company. Chores like radio work on what are called dealer-commercials, the sole purpose of which is to back-up a major seasonal advertising campaign. What that means is this. A series of twenty and thirty-second radio scripts is written and offered, free of charge, to hardware dealers around the country. Time-gaps are left in each script so as to accommodate the dealer's name and address. Individual dealers then approach their local recording studio to have the spots made.

The point of it all is that dealers have the opportunity to identify themselves to the local tool-buying market as Stanley stockists; and it helps to personalize their establishment.

With this to start you off; and with the further information that the exercise is to promote Christmas sales of Stanley Tools to gift-purchasers before and around Yuletide, it's all yours. The market is youngsters and women who may be casting about for something to buy their male relatives and friends. Tool prices in the gift range start at £1.99 for a trimming knife and go up to £23.35 for a bench plane. You already have a comprehensive product-range from the previous script.

Three thirty-second commercials should be sufficient; and the treatment is a single voice-over presentation. My own endeavours appear in Chapter 12.

Don't moan, this is a big account. And don't forget to leave breaks for dealer identification.

* * *

In the advertising scheme of things, television is certainly the hardest-selling of all the media. There can be no real doubt about that. Television has the benefit of visual stimulation, the attraction of immediacy and the advantage of reaching the audience – the captive audience – when it is most vulnerable: when people are relaxed in their own homes. In addition, these people usually view in family groups (people do not normally *read* in family groups); some members of which will be unknowingly working on the advertiser's behalf with expressions of approval like: 'Cor, mum/dad, why haven't we got four of those?' As such, it does a remarkable job.

To my mind, the very best of television – and by that I mean the strongest – is manifested in 'demonstration' advertising. More precisely, that which illustrates the how-it-works-and-why-it-works of a product. Specifically, I call to mind that distinguished piece of work for Volvo which demonstrates the increased engine-power of one of its models by using it to tow a heavily-laden car-transporter. This is an exemplary spot; and thoroughly convincing. Compare it with some of the trendier, glossier examples of car advertising on television, where we are treated to long-legged ladies in surrealistic get-ups and settings, and Volvo comes out a clear winner.

Rule 11   *Advertising that tells you nothing, sells you nothing.*

Filled with rash optimism, I only hope that Volvo will respond equally enthusiastically to this item of buckshee publicity and lose no time in forwarding a free sample of the product.

Rather than involve ourselves, here, with the writing of hundred-thousand pound epics, we will be better employed devising small-budget commercials – since the greater proportion of TV work is exactly that. These days, small-budget could reasonably be determined as anything under £25,000.

So, fine, we are asked to write a low-budget, forty-second spot for an electronic typewriter. The Adivetti. This machine is on a par with the best of electronic typewriters. It uses daisy-wheel printers in a variety of typefaces. It will type both Roman and bold from the same fount. It has a 10K memory and a twenty-character visual display. And it will 'justify' lines left and right.

What makes it a little more interesting than most – and here lies its USP – is that it will convert into a full-blown word-processor by the addition of a compatible, specially-built, screen/interface unit. In this respect, the Adivetti is unique. Also, the typewriter and the Screenprinter-unit together cost about half the price of a regular word-processor.

Whether a product such as this should be on television in the first place is debatable, bearing in mind that the market is likely to be small businesses and, perhaps, journalists and authors. These people are not normally contacted via television so much as by way of the specialist press. What we would, however, be correct in assuming is that this market is already au fait with the concept of word processors and therefore doesn't require a lot of technical detail. All that's really needed is a confident statement that a good word processor is available, and for around half the cost of a standard machine.

The budget we have been allocated for the project doesn't allow the building of magnificent sets or the swanning off to exotic locations. In which case, I suggest we employ some computer graphics. Here's how I would put the script together.

Adivetti	*Forty-second TV*	*VTR*

SFX: MVO, plus synthesizer mood effects to run under

Video	*Audio*
Using computer graphics, we build an Adivetti typewriter line-for-line. As it builds, the image revolves through 360° until the keyboard is facing camera.	1½ seconds mute.
Camera tracks in for MCU. (This sequence shot monochrome.)	MVO: 'So you reckon the last thing you need is a word processor. All right, that's today . . . What about tomorrow?
Dissolve through for matching shot of a full-colour typewriter. (Match dissolve.)	Wouldn't it be better to hedge your bets and have the best of both worlds?
Cut to blank sheet of paper in	You can do just that – and cheaply, too – with an Adivetti

Video	*Audio*
the typewriter. The machine now types the word ADIVETTI in caps, line spaces, then types ADIVETTI in all of the various daisy-wheel typefaces – justifying them as it does so.	electronic typewriter.
	An Adivetti can do everything an ordinary typewriter can do – and then some.
Maybe also a little business with self-correction and the visual display, etc.	You see, an Adivetti adds on. . . .
Now split-screen two ways, retaining the typewriter in the left-hand frame. (MCU.)	You build it into a word processor as and when you're ready.
In the right-hand frame we run a computer graphics sequence and build a Screenprinter. Again to revolve 360°. (Shoot monochrome.)	You simply add our unique screenprinter.
Dissolve through for matching shot of full-colour Screenprinter.	What's even better, the complete unit costs about half what you'd pay for a custom-built machine.
Now integrate both frames to full-frame for *in situ* arrangement of both machines. (MCU.)	
Track in on Screenprinter screen for ECU of cursor and Super appearing letter-for-letter on screen:	
ADIVETTI. THE TYPEWRITER THAT BUILDS INTO A WORD PROCESSOR . . . HALF-PRICE	Adivetti. The typewriter that builds into a word processor . . . for around half the normal cost.'

No question, there are too many words here. I reckon we could omit upwards of a dozen of them without losing the overall message. But as a first-draft it will do. As you can see, too, it's not a shooting script. Writing one would entail the timing of the separate sequences, balancing them with each other, and integrating them to achieve a smooth visual flow.

Incidentally, the one-and-a-half seconds mute, i.e. no sound, at the beginning of the piece is mandatory in all cases.

The following is a short list (a very short list) of various television-production terms and abbreviations, along with their meanings:

Boom shot The camera is mounted on a movable arm to achieve simultaneous tracking, panning and above-and-below eye-level sequences.

Cut Instant change of scene.

Dissolve The image is dissolved out and the following scene dissolved in at the same time.

ECU Extreme close-up.

Freeze frame The freezing of an image and effectively producing a still photograph.

Iris in/out The image is brought into view (or out) by means of dilating or closing the lens.

Match dissolve The image is dissolved from the subject to the same subject in a different location.

MCU Medium close-up.

Soft cut Where two scenes are briefly superimposed – the second slowly taking prominence.

Pan Camera scans the subject from left to right, or vice-versa.

SFX Sound effects.

Super Superimposing words over the image.

Tracking shot Where the camera moves along a track parallel to, towards, or away from the subject.

VO Voice over.

Wipe Changing from one scene to another without cutting. The image is 'blacked out' by panning the camera on to a black object.

Zoom Changing quickly from distance to close-up.

To end this necessarily brief chapter on radio and television, I will mention very quickly that coexistent promotional medium – the audio-visual presentation.

As an advertising tool, the audio-visual has its limitations, but its usefulness as a briefing aid for company sales people or for presenting complicated sales messages to clients, cannot be denied.

Audio-visuals can be produced in a variety of ways, the most common of which are via (a) non-broadcastable video-tape cassettes and (b) slide carousels.

From the writer's point of view, audio-visuals allow a fair degree of self-indulgence, seeing as how they can run from a few minutes to an hour or so. There aren't too many of the latter, however.

By way of demonstrating script layout, I reproduce the opening pages of an audio-visual written for the manufacturer of an industrial pipe-sealing compound:

Slide 1	WL GORE (logo).
Slides 2–7	(Six slides. Each carrying a single letter. Popped-on to spell Gore-Tex.)
Slide 8	Gore-Tex (logo).
VO	'Once upon a time there was no such thing as Gore-Tex.'
Slide 9	Cartoon of caveman – complete with leopard skin, busily chipping a wheel out of stone.
VO	'In fact, there was no such thing as a gasket, even. . . . Had you said to Og, the pithecanthropoid, what's a gasket?, he would have replied: 'How do I know from a gasket, man . . .?'
Slide 10	Cartoon of caveman drawing a mathematical formula on cave wall.
VO	'I'm still working on hang-gliders, man.'
Slide 11	Cartoon cavemen rigging up piping (plumbing?) around cave.
VO	'But there's no denying progress; and one day some bright spark hit on a way of moving liquids from one point to another point without using a bucket.'
Slide 12	Cartoon caveman 'plumbing-in' (i.e. connecting up to a river.)

VO	'Inventing, in the so doing, that remarkable piece of concomitant technology – the leak!'
Slides 13–19	Movie stills of leak situations. (Chaplin, Laurel and Hardy, Buster Keaton, etc.)
VO	'Over the years, leaks have come in all shapes and sizes and in all manner of materials. Water leaks. Gas leaks. Air leaks. Oil leaks. Petrochemical leaks. . . .'
Slide 20	Cartoon or picture of massive, prize (vegetable) leek.
VO	'And leaks of such mammoth proportions that the owners have been elevated. . . .'
Slide 21	Cartoon or picture of explosion – with a body rising in the air.
VO	'To unbelievable heights.'
Slide 22	Movie still of Boris Karloff-type in laboratory surrounded by retorts, beakers, glass tubing, etc.
VO	'And, thus, was invented – the gasket.'
Slide 23	The gasket.
VO	'The gasket.'
Slides 24–32	Actual pictures of the various types of gasket. (Asbestos paper, asbestos cloth, rubber, spiral wound, sheet TFE, braided TFE.)
VO	'Over the years, we've seen asbestos paper; asbestos cloth, rubber and cork – or similar elastomer, spiral wound gaskets, sheet TFE, braided TFE, and envelope gaskets of asbestos and TFE.'
Slide 33	Composite picture of all gaskets mentioned.
VO	'Each in their own way right for the time and efficient to a point.'
Slide 34	Composite picture of Hermetite pack, a

perished rubber gasket, a pile of TFE with flag
embedded announcing: Waste; various gasket
shims; a Stanley knife and a *tin of sticking
plaster*.

VO   'And then, along came Gore-Tex expanded
PTFE – which, if it wasn't a cliché, we would
announce as a second industrial revolution.'

Slide 35   Picture of full range of Gore-Tex joint
sealants.

And so on, and so on . . .

Summary

1   Donkey's years ago, I played drums in a couple of small,
semi-pro jazz combos. Max Roach and Buddy Rich were
my idols; and I came close to selling my soul on a couple
of occasions for the opportunity to 'sit-in' with some of
the luminaries of the British jazz scene.

   As it turned out, I wasn't much of a drummer, but all
those late-night gigs left me with more than just a green
sun-tan. They endowed me with a sense of rhythm and
timing that I otherwise wouldn't have had, and which
has stood me in excellent stead where radio and
television scripting is concerned.

   That the timings of radio and TV scripts must be
nothing less than spot-on goes without saying. Of equal
significance is the rhythm you bring to your phrasing.

   Listen to a good political speaker and you will not fail
to hear the 'rule of three'. In bashing home his various
messages, he will invariably point-up each argument
with a three-phase conclusion: 'I'll say this much. With
no deterrent, there's no security – no way!'

   Now I'm not advising for one minute that your radio
and TV scripts should sound like readings from *Hansard*.
But if you take a close look at the scripts we've cobbled

together in this chapter, you will see numerous examples of the 'triple tonguing' I'm talking about.

Quite clearly, too, the most experienced of voice over artists will be hard-pressed to inject rhythm into the delivery of a script unless you take the trouble to put it there in the first place.

2 In a complicated script, where three or four sales-points have to be aired, it's essential to make each separate component an entity in itself. Each unit should be complete in itself – and not rely on any other unit for balance – yet it should slot into the whole in rather the same way as the middle-eight of a piece of music slots in. You *know* it's an independent element, but you can't hear the join.

3 Some television commercials go out of their way to annoy me. They probably do it deliberately and with intended malice.

They take cliché to the point of embarrassment; and they honour puerility by hanging it on the back of a national advertiser.

Witness the recent series for British Airways which, in one of its offerings, had a stewardess flying around completely unaided and generally behaving like one of those cloaked super-heroes from a bad fifties movie. With all that money to spend, one would have thought that the film-makers could at least have got the back-projection looking right. As it stood, it was amateur-night.

But, then, so is the whole concept. What the air-travelling public thought of it all, I can only guess. I could tell you what the cabin-crews thought, but the law on obscenity precludes it.

How did this silly idea get past first-base? Or, indeed, past the first paper-shredding machine? All it achieves, to my mind, is to make BA look like a bunch of BFs.

By striking contrast, take the campaign of a while ago

for Radio Rentals. The 'Heathcliffe', the 'Submarine', etc. It was bright, it was fresh, and it had all the constituents for lasting memorability.

At a guess, I would say that both these projects enjoyed approximately the same production budgets. So I am not being unfair in making the comparison. Neither am I being one-sided by ignoring the enormously different markets that each is aiming at. Let's look at it in basic terms. If one were to judge purely on the merits of implied authority and responsibility as individually projected by these two companies, I wouldn't mind betting that most people would rather *fly* with Radio Rentals.

It's a classic example of how to let the side down in public. Of how a farcical idea gains respectability by having enormous sums of money poured into it.

What am I telling you? Just this. In television work, by all means be innovative and imaginative. But don't be preposterous, eh?

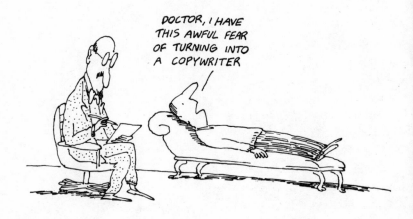

11 Almost final analysis

In this chapter, I shall do no more than reinforce some of the points already discussed and tidy up the loose ends. I rather hope you will read, learn and inwardly digest the following on the grounds that it represents what I see to be the fundamentals of advertising. If you value my opinion at all (though I'm perfectly willing to consider arguments about why you shouldn't – just so long as your letters are accompanied by the equally valid argument of a crisp tenner), you'll do so with some avidity. Because then you'll be as au fait with the basic principles as anyone can be.

Now, you know, as well as I know, that the very sensible, money-spending general public will not beat anything mildly resembling a path to your door unless you have something special to offer. That something special may be as simple as a new kind of coat-hanger, or as complicated as a three-dimensional space-invader machine which propels itself around the country having contests with other three-dimensional space-invader machines. (It could also be a lucid, informative and profoundly witty book such as this one, I suppose. But if the public starts beating paths to my door, it had better bring a bottle.) In any event, the overriding criterion is that the 'thing' must be *special*.

That bit of croft-spawned philosophy applies just as readily to the promotion of the product as to the product itself. After all, where would the product be if nobody knew about it? Unsold, is the answer; and mouldering away by the tonne in somebody's cellar, like as not. What, then, makes a piece of advertising special in our interpretation of that word? Is it cleverness? Is it clarity? Brevity? Sex? Conformity? Or is it, when all is said and done, the research which went into the making of it?

Here are thirteen carefully considered arguments in answer to the above and which, if adhered to, should turn all your ads into special ads.

1   *Cleverness or clarity?*

I am certainly a champion of cleverness in ads – provided that it's not the kind of narcissistic cleverness which often results from a writer, a designer or (quite regularly nowadays) a typographer setting out to show the world what a brilliant chap he is. But even more I'm a champion of clarity.

Advertising, as we've said at some turgid length, is a business of communication and persuasion; and perhaps the most carelessly read words in print are those in an ad. Therefore, to put it into words of one syllable – put it into words of one syllable. By all means be as clever as you like; but not at the expense of making your message clear to people who will be reading it, if you're very lucky, with only half an eye and only a quarter of their attention.

Clarity, without doubt, is the greatest single virtue an ad can have.

2   *A pint jug holds no more than a pint*

One of the worst enemies of clarity in advertising is the tendency to want to say too much. This is not, decidedly not, a condemnation of long copy; on the contrary, I approve of

long copy but with the proviso that it's good long copy –
which it mostly isn't. What I condemn is the attitude of mind
which insists that everything favourable about a product
must be said, however marginal it may be. Lord help us,
most of our potential customers don't give a hoot about our
main sales arguments, let alone the fringe ones.

If, then, you have an ad which features half-a-dozen sales
points, try revising it to feature two of them – and talk three
times as much about each. Or, maybe even better make it
just one and write copy six-fold.

Follow?

3 Hyperbole is a long word

Few copywriters lie. Some exaggerate; and far too many
overstate. But the average manufacturer has a mental block
against saying that his product is only a modest 'good' or
even 'better than most'; he must, he feels, say 'best'. The
copywriter, therefore, in striving to give the client what he
wants, follows suit. Yet, in the following, he does nobody any
favours – least of all his client.

It is a fact of life that the more you use superlatives the less
superlative they become. Hitting somebody over the head
with a bar of iron now and again is fine in its own way; but if
you club him too often he becomes unconscious. The great
Dr Johnson once advised an aspiring writer to go through
what he had written and, when he came to a phrase that
pleased him mightily, to strike it out.

I would advise you to do much the same to the superlatives in your copy.

4 Who's the arbiter of funny?

Nothing is weaker than a weak joke. Alternatively, nothing is more universally penetrative than a good one. Do you, hand on heart, know the difference? And can you honestly judge the reception you'll get when delivering a punchline to a given audience – even an audience you know well?

My advice is: when in doubt, play it straight. Nobody, but nobody, deals with idiots. But if your doubt is marginal, take heart from the fact that the campaigns which are re-membered best have, very largely, been the humorous ones.

5   *Keep away from women*

Unless your advertising is selling direct to women, think twice before allowing women into the picture. And if it's a nubile little creature with not a lot on, think three times. If you can't dream up anything more pertinent to say or to show about a product than the irrelevance of a tight sweater, then resign the account. Or just resign.

6   *Research isn't definitive*

Advertising research, particularly that onerous pre-public-ation copy-testing lark, is a vastly inexact skill. It has much in common with palmistry and water-divining.

By all means spend a little time studying research if the spirit moves you, or if your bosses insist. But simply because you have spent compulsory time on it, and because it emanates from what others consider to be a luminary in the research firmament, don't then treat it as holy writ. Remind yourself frequently that it may turn out to be completely and ludicrously wrong.

To illustrate the mind-blowing negativeness of research, let me quote some recent findings of a Madison Avenue research company. One bright morning, for reasons best known to themselves, they decided to quantify what they were happy to call 'spurious awareness' in the consuming public. Out on to the street they went, en-clipboard-masse; and they questioned the passing populace about three particular products. It turned out that eight per cent of the people they interviewed had heard of a beverage called Four O'clock Tea; sixteen per cent said they knew about Leone Pasta; and some thirty-one per cent was aware of Mrs Smith's Cake Mix.

You won't be at all surprised, I imagine, to learn that all three products were totally fictitious. You may, however, raise an eyebrow when I tell you that, according to the researchers, this piece of research proved that spurious awareness was a factor which should be taken into account during all future research programmes. They reasoned, believe it or not, that spurious awareness would help make research even more scientific and even more accurate.

Have you ever heard the laughable like? It sounds to me like a good case for the nearest asylum.

Has it never occurred to these statistics-wielding lulus that they are having their legs unmercifully pulled? Do they not know that when people are button-holed on the street by strangers with time-wasting questions, they will mostly say the first thing that comes into their head?

It may have struck you, like it has me, that the concept of spurious awareness is, in itself, very, very spurious. It begins with a figment of the imagination on the part of the researchers, and it results in a lie, conscious or otherwise, on the part of those questioned.

The Monty Python team in all its genius could not have devised a more absurd scenario. But that's research for you – so beware.

Research should be viewed with the same circumspection that one would present to some old chap with a conical hat and a beard who told you he could transmute mercury into gold.

7   *One critical swallow doesn't make a summer*

Assume that, with lots of fiery enthusiasm in your belly, you write a slightly contentious ad and, in a moment of insobriety, the client approves it and let's it run. Fifteen million readers do not write to him criticizing it. Three readers do. Should you be swayed by the client's opinion that the offending piece be revised before the next insertion? Alas, you'll probably have small option – though you can put up one almighty fight. And should.

If you believe in what you're doing (and if you don't, why are you doing it?) then try not to succumb to the first choleric gentleman from Cheltenham Spa who writes to say that, in his ill-considered opinion, you are vastly in error.

8   *Logos and taglines never sold anybody anything*

This, I admit, is too sweeping a statement to be wholly true. But it's true enough for all practical purposes.

For those of you who wouldn't know a logo from a rubber-duck, a logotype is that graphic device which appears at the bottom of an ad (usually far too prominently) and which, presumably, is meant to give the reader a neat, symbolic representation of the company to store in his mind and take away with him. Taglines are designed, similarly, to reinforce the image of the product or the company – so they're warm, comforting and often patronizing statements with which to put the ad to bed. They also appear at the tail-end of the ad.

Only a tiny minority of taglines have any memorability, though. I quote: *World's most experienced airline. The best tools you can lay hands on. Better by design. Afore ye go. The appliance of science.* They seem to qualify as having the right ingredients for memorability, on account of I remember them. Even so, taglines are not a 'stop me and buy one' the way headlines are, or should be. Yet, and I speak from experience, once conceived and approved, both logos and taglines become sacred cows. They must always go into any ad and they must never be touched or otherwise adulterated. Like Frankenstein's monster, they develop a life and will of their own; and like them, they shamble around strangling perfectly good layouts, frightening designers and hypnotizing clients.

If people, and by that I mean clients, would only keep taglines and logos in their place, employing them where they are useful and discarding them when they are not, I wouldn't have a word to say against them. But they won't, so I have.

Not everyone, for a change, will agree with me on this. I propose, therefore, to give you a little quiz. This is partly to prove that I am right and partly because it will give you something to do over the weekend.

The following, then, are all slogans in current use. How many advertisers or products can you name? The answers are given below – but try not to cheat, eh?

1 *Honestly made, honestly better.*
2 *The big one.*
3 *The leaders in car care.*
4 *A touch of blue does it.*
5 *You don't have to hope for the best.*
6 *Now is the time.*
7 *Everyone's local building society.*
8 *The margarine for men.*
9 *The best for less.*
10 *Beyond the limits of time.*
11 *The world's favourite airline.*
12 *All together, better.*
13 *Very special cognac.*
14 *One instinctively knows when its right.*
15 *Everyone wants them. We've got them.*

Before anyone runs away with the idea that I may have selected this little lot for their charm, charisma or advertising appeal, allow me to disillusion them. Among the above are some of the worst examples of what I've been telling you not to do for the last 54,000 words, or so. In truth, I find merit in only a very few of them – and remarkably little even then.

1   Robertson's jam.
2   Texas Superstores.
3   Holts car care products.
4   Regal cigarettes.
5   Thomson Travel.
6   Toyota cars.
7   National and Provincial.
8   Flora.
9   Boots Chemists.
10 Citizen watches.
11 British Airways.
12 Asda Superstores.
13 Hennessy.
14 Croft Original Sherry.
15 Minolta Zoom Copiers.

That last one beats all, doesn't it? All I can say is that had I been the client, I should be wondering right now whether my money couldn't be better spent at a crooked casino. Ah, well. . .

Marking? Oh, all right. If you answered five correctly you're on a par with the rest of us around the office – a decent average. Ten, then you certainly keep your eyes open. Many more than that and some agency would be wise to snap you up immediately.

9   *Fashionable advertising doesn't always mean good advertising*

From time to time, one looks up from one's everyday affairs

to be all of a sudden confronted by a new and universal vogue in advertising. I would point to the current trend in cigarette ads and posters as an example.

Just now, almost every cigarette campaign is as near identical to every other cigarette campaign as really doesn't matter. Beautifully designed, they may very well be. Excellently drawn and photographed, they very definitely are. But different they most decidedly ain't. What does that mean? It means that by being in vogue they defeat their own purpose – which is to stand out from the crowd, to be noticed, remembered and acted upon.

Fashion in advertising is an enigma. People create it to be adventurously different from the next bloke's material. But one wrong word down the Charing Cross Road and everybody's at it. How come, you ask, knowing full well how come. Because they want to be in fashion and – wait for it – adventurously different. It's the same the whole world over; in donning the fashionable, they slip into the uniform. This is known, or will be known from henceforth, as the uncreative circle. I may even frame a law about it and, with typical modesty, name it Quinn's conundrum of inventive conformity.

Much of today's booze advertising seems to be similarly afflicted, albeit a little less surrealistic in art direction; and I refer to Scotch in particular. I'm talking more specifically about big-name Scotch, such as one could reasonably demand from a normal off-licence or pub, and not these esoteric malts, dews and creams which they distil in the back-end of the Highlands and purvey only to blood relatives and dear friends. They are, as I say, very much of a muchness. A nicely photographed bottle, a nicely photographed crystal glass, a bland phrase calculated to offend no one, and a tagline similarly sedative is what they consist of. It's 'name' advertising at its flattest; a classic example of how to spend a lot of money to very little effect.

Agreed, the restrictions on spirit and cigarette advertising are manifold. Also agreed, the very many moral and social issues raised by both products preclude the employment of emotive messages. Could it have been done, I should long ago have written a whisky campaign which told the punters in no uncertain terms that imbibing the stuff makes you devastatingly attractive to women, and gives you the financial clout of a Francis Albert Sinatra. But it couldn't and that's that.

My view is that the people who copy vogues are not doing their jobs properly.

And there the matter, whatever it is, rests for the moment.

10   *The confidence trick has no place in advertising*

I recently had the privilege of staying in an hotel not two hundred miles from the heart of England – which should serve to pinpoint its location pretty precisely.

I spent a sultry hour or two in a bar without character where the absence of ice matched the indifference of the service, and had waited several years for a dinner which turned out to be wholly inedible.

Soberly unhappy, I was pacing up and down like a caged mouse in my four-by-two room (where the wash-basin was cleverly placed so as to make it virtually certain that you splashed the bed every time you so much as trickled the tap over a toothbrush) when my eye fell upon the hotel brochure.

I picked it up. Hungry for reading matter, I read it. There, as cool as you like, was the startling assertion that the hotel in question offered '*new concepts of luxury and amenities*'. There was plenty more of the same ilk.

Now literary licence is one thing; and a spot of exaggeration here and there never hurt anyone. But this was not literary licence, nor was it a matter of overstating an already substantial case. It was a brobdignagian lie which would almost certainly have given pause to the great Baron Munchhausen himself.

This kind of hyperbole, which masquerades as advertising copy, is as common in industrial and consumer ads as it is in hotel booklets or the extravaganzas of holiday brochures. Maybe it's even commoner. I shouldn't be at all surprised.

All moral issues aside, there are, as I see it, two main reasons for restraining yourself from over-exaggerating your claims. The first is that you probably won't be believed. The second is that, if you *are* believed, you will be quickly found out to be a liar.

Were I you, I'd look up hyperbole in the dictionary right away; and while you're at it, look up its opposite. It's called meiosis. And it's not used half as much as it should be.

11   Tums and bits – the popularizing of the four-letter word

It all started way back in the late sixties, when the entire world appeared to have lost its marbles, when a great number of people were turning on, dropping out, swapping partners, making love not war, and generally being 'with' a thing called 'it'.

Thoroughly modern, they all thought they were; but thoroughly depressing to blokes like me who had long ago realized that without a certain degree of self-discipline everything becomes a shambles and we all might just as well pour woad over ourselves and take up residence in damp caves.

Coincidental with this era came the 'let's say it like it is' brigade in advertising. 'Let's,' they said, giggling behind their hands, 'say cobblers.' 'Let's follow that with rollocks,' they chimed, having won applause in some quarters for cobblers. This was followed swiftly by tit, bum, pillock and balls. All of these words, these bike-shed words, have been used over the last twenty years in ad headlines.

Good, earthy words, all of them, and terms that many of us use repeatedly every day when we are feeling in a particularly restrained mood. But at the risk of sounding even older and even more prissy than I have done so far, these are expressions which are acceptable when you hear them, but which grate when you read them – especially in ads.

Advertising copy should, at its best, sound like one human being speaking to another. And people talking together do not commonly employ the polished style of Henry James. Nevertheless, any salesman who used the proper equivalent of 'rollocks' to several million people without having met a single one of them would be either an exceptionally good, exceptionally self-confident salesman – or an exceptionally bad one.

This use in advertising print of words and phrases which are normally reserved for casual intercourse among cronies is a habit of which I do not approve. But advertising of this kind is, I suspect and fear, the thin end of what is likely to be a very thick wedge.

I am all for calling a spade a spade; and I am against all the sundry pussyfooting attitudes that, with their hums and ha's and their ifs and buts, can turn a piece of decently straightforward copy into an EEC directive. But if things go on, as I foresee them likely to go on, it won't be long before some bright and probably mistaken spark gets away in a piece of copy with the verbal equivalent of those vastly disappointing scenes in *Deep Throat*.

If you ever feel the need to use a four letter word in copy, I would suggest you choose the far more emotive and sales-getting 'free'.

Anyone who knows me will tell you that I can be as voluble as the next bloke. But I am always well aware beforehand that my audience will accept my vulgarities. To chuck four-letter words at the wrong audience exhibits a lack of courtesy, a want of finesse and a dearth of imagination. Also, in their own peculiar way, those eff and blind words have their own peculiar values. So let us not devalue them.

12   Conversational copy – small talk or selling dialogue?

I notice that more and more writers are using dialogue in press copy. You know the sort of thing. There's a picture of the managing director waving a stern finger at the sales manager, and he's saying, more or less: 'Now look here, Charles, if we don't deliver those parts to Messrs Cranshawes in Somerset by the morning, we'll lose the entire order.' But Charles, being nobody's old mug, has the whole situation buttoned up: 'I've already sent them off with Express Despatch – they'll deliver on time.' Yes, you do know the sort of thing.

Used in strip-cartoon form, conversational copy is quite effective – if a touch puerile in the eyes of some markets. However, when dialogue is translated into the body copy of an ordinary ad, complete with para indents, speech marks, dialectal language and all, things usually take a turn for the idiotic. It's difficult enough writing dialogue in novels, where you have all the space and, therefore, all the opportunity in the world to explore every thought at great length. But in ads, where space is strictly limited, the sell has to be developed with some immediacy. This usually results in conversation so contrived that no human being would be capable of delivering it. Which has the result that no human being is prepared to believe it.

What am I trying to tell you? Should you avoid conversational copy like the small-pox. Not at all. But always remember there is a certain thing called immunization.

13   Radio and television – the basic principles apply

We've spoken very little about radio and television advertising; and for good reason. Just because I won a Grand Prix at the Cork Film festival (for Kerrygold butter – and, I believe, the only one held this side of the Atlantic); it doesn't follow that I am by any means an authority. But, very largely, all I have said about the fundamentals of press copy applies in this area also.

If you are fortunate, if you have an ear and an eye for it, you will be invited to studios to see your work produced. Indeed, you may even get the opportunity to produce the material yourself – which is a chance you should unreservedly take. Working with professional voice over artists, broadcasting personalities and musicians is a most rewarding experience. You will come to discover that these people may take a different view of that deathless script you put together back in the office. You will very quickly learn that whatever you write can be interpreted in a dozen different ways. You will come to realize that subtle script changes, vocal inflection and pace of delivery can give lift to even the dullest of scripts. And when you work with certain artists on a regular basis, you will write specifically for their voices.

But whether you're working with a big name or a sixty-quid-an-hour voice over hack, always keep it in the back of your mind that both have probably forgotten more about microphone technique and camera presentation than you are ever likely to learn.

Rule 11   *A good copywriter is someone who does unique things of which nobody would expect him capable.*

12   Exercise conclusions

Press exercise conclusions from chapter 7

I'll run through this exactly as each thought hit the button.
I've made just a few attempts in each case – but that doesn't
mean that *you* shouldn't do at least a dozen of each. The first,
the Z60 typewriter.

Exercise 1

£190 SAYS YOU CAN WRITE

A BEST SELLER

Or perhaps:

INSTANT AUTHORSHIP: £190

Better still:

THE Z60 GIVES YOU FREELANCE FREEDOM

WITH PROFESSIONAL RESULTS

FOR JUST £190

The copy almost writes itself:

The Z60 is what you might call the definitive portable typewriter.

In fact, it's the first ever completely cordless electronic typewriter.

It's small enough to use on the plane, train or bedside table. And light enough to go anywhere you go.

Versatile? Certainly! There's a choice of type styles. Plus a fifteen-character display and a one-line memory – to help prevent mistakes.

And to put them right when they happen.

Etc.

The final line could read something like this:

We're not saying you'll always get published. But you'll always get read.

And now to the Vulcan 10 copier.

Exercise 2

THE VULCAN 10

IS MADE FOR SMALL BUSINESSES

YOU COPY?

Alternatively:

THE VULCAN 10 IS DESIGNED

FOR SMALL BUSINESSES . . . SMALL

BUSINESSES . . . SMALL BUSINESSES . . .

The latter is more for fun than for a serious sales pitch, so we had better take the whole thing a mite more soberly:

SMALL BUSINESSES ARE MULTIPLYING
RAPIDLY WITH THE VULCAN 10 COPIER

With appropriate copy, of course.

The Vulcan 10 is one of the smallest and lightest plain-paper copiers on the market.

It's just 20 inches by 20 inches by 8 inches and weighs under 8 lbs.

Yet it produces up to 2000 perfect copies at one loading.

Which makes it ideal for small business premises.

Or for people working from home.

And the Vulcan 10 is as versatile as they come.

Because it not only reproduces in five different colours. But also copies on to any kind of paper.

On tissue. Bond. Bank. Even on wrapping paper . . .

Exercise 3

Which brings us, finally, to the Cogent 11 calculator. My contribution runs thus:

THE COGENT 11.
DOES MORE THAN A CALCULATOR.
COSTS LESS THAN A COMPUTER

Along with:

THE COGENT 11. A SMALL-BUSINESS
COMPUTER AT A SMALL-BUSINESS PRICE

If the client will wear it, we might suggest:

HOW TO RUN A ONE-MAN BAND
AND NEVER FORGET THE SCORE

Or maybe:

THE MAGNUM OPUS
FOR ONE-MAN BANDS

But I much prefer either of the following:

INSIDE EVERY COGENT 11 SMALL BUSINESS
COMPUTER
THERE'S A BIG BUSINESS BRAIN

And:

A BIG-BUSINESS COMPUTER
FOR AROUND HALF
THE COST?

THAT'S ABOUT THE SIZE OF IT

(Picture: Cogent 11 in the palm of a hand.)

The Cogent 11 is our way of putting a full-scale computer into the hands of the small-business user.
Literally.
Can't afford a computer? Oh, yes you can.
Because the Cogent 11 costs around half the price of a conventional computer.
Yet it can handle all your business affairs. From stock control to sales projections.
From invoicing to profit and loss accounts.
Just like the one you can't afford.
You simply plug into an ordinary TV screen for a full visual display of 90 characters by 24 lines. And any

compatible printer will take full advantage of the 64K memory . . .

Exercise 4

Trans-National Coaches. Here we go:

GONE ARE THE DAYS WHEN
YOU COULD TRAVEL FROM
LONDON TO EDINBURGH FOR £11

TRUE OR FALSE?

False.

The single fare from London to Edinburgh by a Trans-National coach is just £11.

Considerably less than you pay for any other kind of public transport.

In fact, it's £24 cheaper than rail. And a full £84 less than by air.

We take you to Edinburgh every day. Twice a day.

We pick you up from literally dozens of stops in London en-route. And we put you down in Edinburgh. Safe and sound.

Our coaches are modern and always spick and span. You travel in comfort — with reclining seats, and personal lighting and heating system. The seating arrangement gives you plenty of room to stretch out and relax.

Trans-National Coaches. We go all the way for £11. And we'll bring you back for only £22.

For all the facts on fares . . .

Some alternative headlines could take the following shape:

IT'S AMAZING HOW FAR

SOME PEOPLE WILL GO

TO SAVE £84

Or, preferably:

THERE'S ONLY ONE WAY TO TRAVEL

TO EDINBURGH

CHEAPER THAN TRANS-NATIONAL

(Picture: large pair of scruffy training-shoes – with feet inside – and which appear to have done a lot of walking.)

We might even employ these same shoes with a line saying:

THE CHEAPEST WAY TO TRAVEL

FROM LONDON TO EDINBURGH

(Now a picture of a Trans-National coach.)

THE SECOND CHEAPEST

Infinitely better is this long, but not overlong, headline that explains the entire story:

FOR £11 BY TRAIN, YOU MIGHT MAKE

WATFORD.

BY AIR, YOU'D GET AS FAR AS THE END

OF THE RUNWAY.

BUT FOR THE SAME MONEY, WE'LL TAKE

YOU ALL THE WAY TO EDINBURGH

* * *

Script exercise conclusions from chapter 10

The exercise was to write 3×30 second scripts for Stanley tools, each promoting hand-tools as Christmas presents, each using a male voice over.

Script 1

> *MVO to be delivered as a send-up of 'ministerial-spokesman' type bulletins. Officious, haughty and rather idiotic.*

MVO: 'Good day. I am the official spokesman for Christmas; and I can now tell you that Christmas will definitely be happening *again* this year.

   So all of you mums, aunts, sisters, wives and mothers-in-law had better pop into Jason Mason's Hardware Store, Two Cubes Avenue, Dyce for presents of super Stanley tools, for dads, brothers, sons and . . . hum . . . lovers. That's Jason Mason's Hardware Store, Two Cubes Avenue, Dyce for the finest selection of Stanley tools in town. So there you are, then, your Christmas gift ideas all wrapped up for another year.

   And that's official.'

Script 2

> *MVO is a 'close-to-mike', throaty voice with lots of timbre. Delivery is a send-up of those unctuous headache-remedy commercials.*

MVO: 'The man in your life – is he listless, inattentive . . . boring?

   Then get him a really worthwhile Christmas gift

this year. Buy him something from the vast range of Stanley tools at Jason Mason's Hardware Store, Highwayman Road, Andover.

Prices start at under £2.

Yes, gifts from the Stanley tool range at Jason Mason's Hardware Store, Highwayman Road, Andover mean that your man can now do all those long-awaited DIY jobs around the home.

And that should get him back on his feet again. Even if . . . it's only . . . to leave home.'

Script 3

A gushing female voice over, à la the new breed of TV and radio Agony Aunt. Lots of 'chin-up, it's not as bad as you think, girls' inflection.

FVO: 'Hello, everybody – it's me again.

Tell me, what will you be giving the chap in your life this Christmas?

A tie? A pair of socks? A season-ticket to the local? Now that's not very imaginative, is it? Take my tip, pop into Jason Mason's Hardware Store in Centipede Road, Crawley and get him something from the simply wonderful range of Stanley tools.

The address once again: Jason Mason's Hardware Store, Centipede Road. It's a Stanley tools cornucopia.

Of course, there's a method to all of this.

He can't build your new kitchen units with a pair of socks – can he, my dear?'

Except for one instance, I have deliberately neglected to mention prices. This is because I doubt the usefulness of nominating prices in radio commercials. The practice may be tolerable where one product and, therefore, one price is involved; but I maintain that listeners will not absorb them in quantity. Televison gets away with it, of course, on the grounds that the prices are also visually displayed – which aids memorability. Even so, I'm not crazy about the idea.

So there you have it. I trust that you are happier with your efforts than you are with mine? Well, that's exactly the way it should be.

13   Getting the job and keeping it

I rather hope that, by now, you will have a better than fair idea of what it takes to lift copy-work out of the ordinary. I shall be pleased, too, if even the well-initiated have gained something from the preceding pages. But what of those who aren't gainfully employed in a copy-shop? What exactly does it take to land that elusive job?

The way I see it is that, first, you must have a genuine understanding of what has already been said. (Which is the reason I've held this chapter until the end.) And, second, you ought to have some guidance on your methods of approach to prospective employers.

Here it is.

There are close to nine hundred ad agencies in the UK. I also have it on good authority that there exist some three thousand companies possessing substantial in-house publicity/marketing departments – all of whom, at one time or another, initiate copywriting. This material either comes from within, or from freelance sources. Couple these with several thousand freelance design groups and freelance copy outfits, and you have a sizeable market in which to tout your services.

But hold fast. It's a sad fact of life that the chances of being taken on by any of them, unless you have some experience, are not good. Just as maddening, you can't expect to have experience unless someone employs you and gives you the chance to gain it.

It's the classic catch 22. But let's be honest, you'll hit the same basic snag no matter what new line of employment you go after.

Fortunately, things aren't as black as may first appear. There is a workable solution to the problem.

To put it simply, you manufacture your own experience. And you write something which so impresses a third-party that they feel unable to operate without you.

How do you do that? First, you consider enrolling on a communications course at one of the very many colleges of further education. If you're within travelling distance of Watford, you are fortunate, indeed, since Watford College, in Hempstead Road, runs a first-rate, full-time copywriting programme. But, as I say, many other splendid establishments organize advertising, marketing and copy courses. For a full list of where, when and how much they cost, drop a line to: the Council for National Academic Awards, 344–354 Gray's Inn Road, London, WC1 8BP. Or the Business and Technician Education Council, Berkshire House, 168–173 High Holborn, London, WC1V 7AG. Or the Communication, Advertising and Marketing Education Foundation Limited, Abford House, 15 Wilton Road, London, SW1V 1NJ. In Scotland, you should apply to: the Scottish Business Education Council, Great King Street, Edinburgh.

Next, you begin subscribing to the professional advertising and marketing magazines. Start with *Campaign* – you'll find it at all good high street booksellers – then progress from there. Over a period, you will gather a general picture from the information therein of which agencies are doing what for whom, where, and for how much. You will glean the names of agencies, personalities, advertising budgets, and be privy to the analysis of current ad campaigns. In short, you will receive a thorough grounding on the advertising scene as it stands right now.

Obviously, you will also engross yourself deeply in the situations vacant columns to discover the going rates, the salaries in various areas for junior, middleweight and senior writers. The help wanted ads will also spell out exactly what the agencies expect for their money.

During this period, you should carry out some in-depth research on the agencies in your immediate locale. This is a piece of cake and can be easily accomplished by paying a visit to your local public library. Ask for the *Advertising Blue Book*. It's a reference work, so you won't be able to take it away. However, the *Blue Book* lists every recognized agency in Britain and Eire. It also details each agency's full client list. More pertinent, from your point of view, is the fact that it also gives a complete rundown on management staff. Including the names of copy chiefs and creative directors.

Arguably, any job-hunter with a name to contact, plus a good background knowledge of the firm he's approaching, will be several lengths ahead of the idle character who has not bothered his head to find out these things.

Having done that, you will reply to every relevant recruitment ad in *Campaign* and your local paper. And you will do so even when they are only looking for a production assistant or a lowly traffic wallah. Because once you're in, you're in – and you'll be better placed to prove what you can do from the inside. You will also begin to frequent the 'advertising' pubs in your area; and the names of every creative director and copy chief of local agencies will be indelibly engraved upon your mind, because one day you are going to bump into them.

The name of that game is research. The third stage is homework. What I mean is that to properly call yourself a writer, you'll have to do some writing.

So write.

Write articles. Write plays. Poetry. Short-stories. Radio talks – anything. Above all, write ads. Set tests for yourself by re-thinking the better ads in the papers. Produce new headlines; crack out new copy; devise new tag-lines.

Right now, in all probability, you are questioning the efficacy of writing the non-advertising material – and why on earth shouldn't you question it? Here's the answer, or rather the answers. First, you're writing to exercise your mind, your vocabulary, and to develop a style. Second, you are doing so in the hope of getting published. Third – and perhaps the noblest reason – because you have come to like it. All of it is geared towards honing your creativity and to eventually having something concrete to present to a future employer.

It's one of the elements of your experience-gathering exercise.

Do not, therefore, allow your efforts to lie around gathering dust. Send them off to publishers and editors; even if the only response you elicit is a swift and uncompromising rejection slip.

A copy chief will look more kindly upon someone who has at least made the effort, whether he has succeeded or not. Whatever the case, you'll have gained the experience of making submissions to publications and possess bundles of typed manuscripts; and that's a talking point any way you look at it. Again, the public library will have a copy of the *Writers and Artists Year Book*, an invaluable reference for determining where and how to sell manuscripts.

It won't be easy in the beginning. Let's be honest about it, getting published is no walkover. Eventually, though, your efforts are bound to be rewarded – perhaps by some poor editor who finds it more expedient to capitulate in the face of your unflagging persistence.

* * *

Very well, you are armed with a dossier of information about the agency you mean to approach. You have all the names of the top people, their positions, and a rundown on the agency's clients. But why have you chosen this agency in particular? You've chosen it because you have seen its work, have heard or read good reports about its managers, and like what you see. You haven't chosen it because it's only a four-penny bus-ride from where you live. I hope not – I sincerely hope not!

You also have a substantial bundle of practice copy, along with other examples of your work – published, or not.

So now you can make your job application pitch (we're assuming, of course, that you haven't suddenly got lucky and been invited to attend an interview as a response to a situations vacant ad.) Are you ready? Fine. *Now make your pitch in writing.*

Try phoning or turning up to see a copy chief or a creative director out of the blue and see what you get. What you'll get is right under his skin. The nett result of which will be a fobbing-off or, at worst, a point-blank refusal ever to see you again. And that's just what you don't want. Clearly, you cannot afford to upset anybody at this stage in the game. So, as mentioned, write; and write direct to the copy chief or the creative director with a request for an interview.

You will also give them information – apart from the obvious things like age, sex, and present occupation – that tells them how you've been working at becoming an agency writer, and why you want to be one. On the latter point, don't mention money. Your reasons should be purely honourable. You are ambitious; you want to make advertising your life's work; and you believe that you can make a very real contribution to the work of the agency.

In your letter, ask whether the agency conducts copy tests; and keep your fingers crossed. On the basis of what you've learned so far, if you are given a copy test, you are as good as employed. Make no mistake about it.

A copy test is an agency's method of sorting the interviewee wheat from chaff. In principle, it's a sound idea; though when you come to do it, be prepared for a good few surprises. For motives which I'll explain, copy tests are almost always larger than life. They are, to put it bluntly, grossly exaggerated examples of a creative brief.

You might, for instance, be set a brief telling you that a certain carbon-paper process has developed a manufacturing fault whereby both sides of the paper are impregnated with carbon. Your job, therefore, is to hit upon a USP likely to shift tons of this largely useless product and knock-up a campaign for launching it upon an unsuspecting market.

Another might be the task of producing a series of ads extolling the virtues and benefits of winter-holidaying on the island of Rockall. And so on.

Why are the briefs so way-out? For psychological rather than practical purposes. Anyone who can write to that kind of scenario can write anything.

Given that you are asked to do a copy test take full advantage of the opportunity. Make up your mind to sit the thing in the agency, you'll probably be given a time limit. So be prepared for that. Most of these exercises, however, are designed to be accomplished over several days in your own home; and that's a far better proposition from your point of view.

But, either way, approach the test methodically. First, put down every thought that occurs to you relative to the brief. Every phrase; every cliché, every slang term, rhyming or otherwise. From this mass of disparate ideas, begin to formulate your headlines. And I don't mean four or five, I mean forty or fifty. Write pages of them; reams if you can. Good, bad or indifferent, it doesn't matter at this stage, just get them down on paper. Leave no stone unturned in your efforts to drain the subject dry. Next, examine the lines carefully. The chances are you will find that they appear to fall into naturally related groupings. This is a not unusual manifestion of the creative process – the brain travels from one idea to the next in a straight line. Every thought is triggered by the one which went before it. All you have to do now is isolate groupings and within each one, somewhere, will lie the most suitable line – or series of lines. You're not finished yet, though. Select the half-dozen lines which appeal to you most and work on them; play with the words, tease more life into the phrases. And while you're at it, ask yourself these questions: Do I need to add a word or two to make the line flow more readily? Will the deletion of a word help clarity? Will it work better if the line is turned completely around? Or by making two sentences from one? Does the inclusion of a hyphen or a three-dot ellipsis help turn two clauses into an easily absorbed statement?

The possibilities and permutations are endless; but don't call a halt until you are convinced that no room remains for improvement.

All right, now write some short introduction copy to each chosen headline. This is to determine whether the gist of the line will easily translate into the text of the ad.

Which brings me to the often disregarded principle that a headline must stand on its own feet – stand or fall on it's own merits.

There is, you will agree, very little point in having to write several paragraphs in order to explain what your headline is all about. The ideal headline – the only headline worthy of the name – is one which speaks for itself, loudly and clearly. You should *never* put yourself into the position where you need to justify the headline. It must always be crisp, precise and very much to the point.

From here on, life becomes a little less tense. You are almost home and dry. Your remaining task is to put down some sticks of solid body copy for each of the selected lines.

Now let me give you a tip.

Some briefs will naturally generate half-a-dozen USPs, each as important as the other. In this circumstance, write an ad for *each* unique selling proposition. In other words, prepare a campaign comprising as many ads as it takes, each majoring on a given selling point. In the case of the Rockall holidays brief given above, these selling points may be: privacy; abundance of wildlife; exclusive resort; limited numbers of holidaymakers on the island; escape from civilization; two sea cruises as part of the holiday package deal (people have to get there and back somehow.)

See what I mean?

The result, whether it's a multi-faceted campaign, or a series of ads, will constitute your main presentation. It should be typed up with great care, using a separate A4 sheet for each ad.

So what do you do with the extraneous material – the headlines that didn't quite make the grade? You keep 'em, you type 'em and present 'em as alternative thoughts. Like that, you'll be doing what agencies themselves do. When presenting creative ideas to clients, the cleverer outfits keep concomitant propositions up their sleeves. And they do so as an insurance against having their initial ideas shot down.

If that happens, the conversation at a presentation will run along these lines:

Client   I can't say that any of your submissions bowls me over. Maybe you should go away and think again.

Agency   Fortunately, we don't have to. The campaign you've just seen was conceived within the strictures of the brief as we saw it. However, we've taken things a stage further and would now ask you to consider this second campaign, which interprets the brief rather more fully, blah, blah blah . . .

The moral is: never discard anything; no matter how banal and puerile it may appear to you. To someone else it might be the definitive work. Good advertising, like beauty, is in the eye of the beholder. That is, of course, until it proves itself in the market-place. And since the beholder is generally the chap who's shelling out good money to put it into the papers, he will be the final arbiter – whether he knows anything about advertising or not.

*   *   *

Let's talk some more about your initial approach to the agency.

In your letter of application, you will very likely be tempted to list all your previous jobs and come clean about your qualifications. That's an honest and agreeable attitude which does you much credit. But will it do you much good?

Do, by all means quote O levels and degrees; and if you are currently employed, say so. But don't under any circumstances list a whole series of jobs that you've walked out of in fits of pique, or go to great lengths over an educational record which amounts, when analyzed, to a handful of nothing.

You must think positively – agencies do. They never speak negatively about themselves. Everything in their respective gardens is lovely. When they go broke and are taken over, they announce a 'merger'; and when they lose an account, they tell the world that they 'resigned' it. Always remember, advertising is all about the art of getting a quart of mileage out of a pint of benefits. So start thinking the way the profession thinks.

If you're unemployed, you may care to call yourself a freelance writer. You have, if you've taken a blind bit of notice of what I've said, been writing – and you've been attempting to get published.

It's no more than the literal truth.

Not for one moment am I suggesting you tell deliberate lies in your letter of application. Nevertheless, you can quite properly embroider the truth so that it shows you to the best advantage. You must use all the ammunition that's available.

Also, take the emotive tack: show willing. I should be far more impressed by someone who told me they had only two O levels, but had cleaned cars or washed dishes in order to pay for further education, than somebody claiming a Ph.D who admitted to doing absolutely nothing for a crust.

While I advise caution, therefore, when talking about

your achievements, a little imagination will give substance to even the most unexciting of them.

Obviously, everything you write should be typed. This also includes your job application. It must be typed on A4 paper and never, ever folded. Send it away, along with anything else you think might interest the agency – sample copy, articles, poems, or even news stories you may have had published in the local press – personally addressed to whoever you wish to contact. And, as I say, don't fold it. Send it in a full-size, A4 buff envelope. It would be wise to include a stamped, self-addressed envelope thus to try to ensure a reply and, hopefully, something more than just a cursory, negative response. The great majority of letters of application to an agency seem to expect a reply as a matter of course, or courtesy. One should not bank on it. The thing to do, if you hear nothing, is to make another pitch; and keep plugging away until their hand is forced, one way or another.

It takes not much effort, either, to make a personalized folder. A sheet of Letraset (those self-adhesive alphabet sheets, obtainable in any art shop) will help no end to dress the folder up. You can even make your own letterhead with Letraset – then have a few run off at the local photocopy shop.

What you're after, here, is impact. Give the impression that you want your work to be seen in the best possible light. Nothing is more delightful to handle – nothing more tactile – than a carefully prepared document; and by that token, the standard of the stuff inside need not be the best in the world. But send ill-draughted work and it will almost certainly not reach your contact's desk – and neither will you. Why give yourself more problems than you already have?

If the foregoing strikes you as a painfully obvious way of going about things, I can only say that you are fortunate in being among the very few who think that way. In truth, nine out of ten aspiring copywriters are totally incapable of presenting themselves or their work with any degree of proficiency. Which is why they mostly fail.

I receive handwritten 'notes' (that's the best way to describe them) which are almost illegible. No care or attention has been given to them whatsoever. I bin them. What would you do? Also, from time to time, I am sent letters that pay me the discourtesy of not even being signed. Some others assume, quite wrongly as it turns out, that I am falling over myself to see what their self-styled genius has wrought. 'I shall be passing your office at ten tomorrow. You can see me then,' they say. 'Oh, no I can't,' I reply; and don't.

One additional thought in this area. Agencies are crying out for new talent. That doesn't mean to suggest that you have to be fresh out of school to qualify; though the 'whizz-kids' put around stories to the contrary, presumably in order to protect their own precarious positions. There are, take my word, any number of middle-aged copywriters hacking it with the best of them. In any event, I was never wholly convinced about the youth-cult, even when people started talking about it back in the fifties when I was a youth myself!

What it does require – and in no uncertain terms – is skill. Not writing skill, nor even academic skill in those terms; but such skill as shows that you can reduce a highly complicated brief to an easy-to-understand sales message of substance.

As you've already seen, that's not so difficult once you apply your mind. Will you apply yours?

I rather hope so.

* * *

A word or two, here, about your tactics once you've got yourself installed behind an agency desk. First, don't just sit there occupying yourself with the arrangement of your pens and pencils – put yourself about. Chat up account executives, fawn on creative directors, and generally make your presence felt and win a reputation. Otherwise, I can assure you, your three-month trial period will gallop past and you will have made little or no impression on anyone. Advertising, you see, is all about impressions; all about image. A trainee copywriter needs publicity every bit as much as any new product.

Thus, when asked – no matter how reluctantly – to sit in on a big briefing meeting, if only as an observer, you will do so with some alacrity. Take your leads from the professionals, meaning those present who are eliciting the most favourable responses from the rest of the crowd; back them up, and chip in with sensible expansions of their ideas. You won't get the credit if any of those thoughts come to fruition, but at this stage simply accept the fact.

Once the meeting is over, once all the responsibilities have been delegated, and once the creative platform for the job has been defined, you will return to your desk and work, work, work. That's what they mean by being a self-starter. The senior writer on the job is the one to whom you should report. And although he will steal your best ideas, he will, at the same time, see you as someone who can bail him out and be something of a life-jacket when things get rough. Thus, you will be a person who, in his view, should be around on a permanent basis; and he will, for purely mercenary reasons, make this view clear to those who matter, which is what I mean by winning a reputation. It's necessary for your survival.

Perhaps the most significant feature of survival in an agency is productivity. By that I mean productivity which allows your time to be re-charged to the client so that even if the agency doesn't make a direct profit from you, at least it won't make a loss.

See it this way. When an agency sits you at a desk and supplies heat, light, cleaning, typewriter, paper, pens and all the accoutrements of civilized working conditions, it does so at a cost. A substantial cost. Add to that your salary and we're talking large sums. All up, we're talking a figure which works out at about twice your wages. So for them to see any daylight at all, you must do enough re-chargeable work per annum to completely wipe out your cost to them.

Many agencies, these days, make sure you're putting in the appropriate amount of graft by asking you to complete a daily time-sheet. These iniquitous documents are then checked every several months, and if the maths aren't up to expectations, you are hauled ignominiously over coals. I dislike time-sheets intensely. They are an abomination unto the copywriter, and a pain in the neck to anyone more interested in knocking out good work than in producing profit. But, to be fair and to be sensible, profit is what agencies are in business to earn – whether it offends the creative sensibility or not.

On that score, it will help no end, when punting for a job, if your line in business patter equals your line in artistic patter. If you can convince an agency that you have a good commercial awareness between your ears, you'll be far more likely to nail down a position than someone who displays a lack of business acumen.

But, anyway, like almost everything else in life, the pursuance of productivity has its snags. The major one of these is the ubiquitous 'meeting'. Now, meetings – the coming together of like-minded souls for a mutual purpose – are as much a part of agency existence as are expense account lunches for account executives and no pay for overtime for creative people. To be sure, many people consider the calling and attending of meetings to be materially more important than the compilation of ads. Needless to point out, these people aren't the ones charged with the task of compiling ads – otherwise they wouldn't spend so much time at meetings. But the poor old copy-writer, if he wants to take a brief and do the job he's paid for, is duty-bound to present himself wherever and whenever called upon so to do.

Thus, it can happen and often does, that you spend entire days ensconced in a variety of offices, chewing a variety of fats. So, obviously, the real writing work fails to get done;

you neglect to fill out an honest time-sheet; and eventually all hell falls upon your neck in the shape of somebody higher up with a hornet-in-his-hat about rechargeable time. Agreed, you can re-charge *some* talking and thinking time, but even the most agreeable of clients is not going to wear an invoice in which the creative charge resembles the national debt.

Your only way out, when meetings appear to be ruling your life, is to do the real work in your own time in the loneliness of your own home. It's good for your job, it's good for your sanity; and I doubt that there is one copywriter in this land who doesn't take his work home with him – in his head, if not on paper. Which, again, is the mark of a true professional.

To sum up, it would be correct to say that a copywriter not only has to justify his existence by what he produces, but also by how profitable or cost-effective he is.

* * *

I am aware that the somewhat tricky job-situation of present times prompts many a young writer to leap straight from college on to the freelance market. I admire them their get-up-and-go, but experience shows that given even the warmest of economic climates, this is never a good idea. And with pennies being pinched black-and-blue, as they are right now, the very brightest of graduates will almost certainly be on a hiding to nothing. Indeed, in punting around looking for commissions, most will find themselves in the same leaky boat as the Flying Dutchman – with identically frustrating results.

To explain why, maybe I should define the role of the freelance writer and describe some of the problems he encounters.

First, the freelance operates in a kind of limbo. Most of his work is executed away from the source of the commission.

Sure, a good few agencies expect him to work *in situ*, as it were; but as things go, he generally functions out of his own premises.

Given this fact, it follows that dialogue is strictly limited. The brief is received at their place, then the writer disappears to try to fulfil it. One or two intermediate phone calls may follow, so as to clarify the odd point, though by and large any to'ing and fro'ing between agency visualizer/ account executive and the freelance will be minimal. What's more, you 'ain't one of them'. Meaning that you're an outsider. And, in so far as the resident writers of said agency are interested, you can damned-well stay that way. Never forget that they may very well be miffed because you were brought in over their heads.

It can be seen from this that the freelance has to be a self-starter who is able to fill gaps in briefs (as there almost always are) with his own well-considered interpretations, and not spend endless hours on the phone posing awkward questions. To do this effectively, he needs more than a modicum of actual brief-cogitating experience. But to get that . . . well . . . new readers start at Chapter 1.

Second the freelance must be a paragon of virtue, and the tightest of tight-lipped characters, who can neither talk about nor take credit for any of the work he does for agencies. A reputation in this respect has to be earned over a period of years – it cannot be gained overnight. So when he freelances for a couple of dozen different agencies, as I do, mum is not only the word, it's the way, the truth and the life.

Agency A must never know what you undertake for agency B. And when B asks you to help with a presentation for an account you already work on for A, you must place your cards firmly on the table and decline. Otherwise, you will not only be in the ludicrous position of pitching against yourself, you will also stand to be dismissed by both A and B when they eventually tumble to your devious little game.

An agency client of mine recently won an equitably

prestigious copy award. They won it for a campaign I had written on behalf of an important emptor of theirs. However, the actual writing credit went to the firm's creative director, with the sop to me that they would have difficulty explaining to their client why they resorted to the use of outsiders. All very understandable, really.

Freelances have to look at it this way. If the agency is tipping up with a fee, who cares who gets the credit?

Not me, for one.

Third, a freelance always operates at the whim of his customers. What I find is that agencies hand out work in waves. For six months, you pick up everything they have to offer. The following six months, you get zilch. Similarly, an agency which has employed you consistently for a number of years, will suddenly drop you like a sack of mangles – and for no apparent reason. Likewise, an agency you have seen neither hide nor hair of for years will all at once request your attendance forthwith. This means dropping everything and getting round there, despite the several other urgent jobs on your desk begging for immediate attention.

When all is said and done, freelancing is no bed of roses; and, as you have seen, not a job that lends itself all that readily to the novice.

But why, you may be asking, if it's so very awful, is *he* doing it? Simple. I am even crazier than I look.

Rule 12   *Beware of pundits bearing rules.*

Epilogue

I rather hope that this book has encouraged you to want to improve your copy skills, or to take up copywriting as a career. If, however, it has turned you off the idea for ever, I can only apologize. If, similarly, I have pontificated too long; and if you now feel like some kind of door that I have had a foot jammed in, I apologize again.

In putting these thoughts together, I have made much of the importance of old-fashioned hard work; and I really cannot overstress my belief that the only way to succeed as a writer is to graft, graft, graft. Putting a novel, a play or an advertising campaign together and believing that the public will be foolish not to recognize your genius is understandable self-delusion. We each do it at one time or another. But if that novel, play or campaign is the only one you ever produce – and if you insist that it's the best you'll ever do – then you are, sir or madam, at odds with the very laws of natural artistic progression. You've got to keep at it whatever your critics may think; and I promise you that every day, in every way, you will get better and better.

To those people who decide to take the plunge and are fortunate enough to find themselves behind an agency desk, I'd like to know how you get on. I should also like to know whether my efforts help you to develop in the job.

Well, if the publisher receives enough kindly comment, he

may very well ask me to write a sequel. And here's your second most important lesson. It concerns the professional copywriter's ability to plan ahead, to pre-empt the client's brief. You see, I already have the sequel drafted.

Glossary of advertising terms

Above the line Pure, media advertising, i.e. press, radio and television.

Account director The agency representative with overall responsibility for the conduct of a given batch of accounts.

Account executive The agency go-between who services the client day-to-day. Sometimes called an account handler.

Advertising manager The client's front-man. It's his job to brief the agency.

Advertising Standards Authority The watchdog body which monitors advertising from a moral and legal standpoint.

Below the line Any promotional material that doesn't qualify as pure media work. Things like promotional literature, incentive give-aways (mugs, key-rings, etc). *See* point of sale.

Brief In essence, the client's instructions to the agency. In reality, an analysis of his product and market, all refined into a working document for interpretation by creative and media personnel.

Budget Or, the 'spend'. The appropriation set aside by the client to meet the cost of campaigns. This includes creative, production and media costs.

Camera-ready *See* finished art.

Campaign A number of different ads doing the same selling job in the same way. Each ad clearly having (by design or copy treatment) the same parentage.

Commercial A television or radio advertising spot. (Calling either of them an ad is a sign of unfamiliarity with the medium.)

Copy chief The manager of the agency copy department. He is answerable to the creative director.

Copy testing A method by which samples of copy are read by selected sections of the public – their reactions are evaluated for market 'appeal'.

Creative director The person responsible for the overall creative performance within an agency.

Designer An artist. Sometimes called a visualizer or an art director.

Direct mail Mailer or mail-shot. Personalized letters, brochures or promotional material sent to prospects through the post.

DPS Double-page spread, i.e. two facing pages in a magazine or newspaper.

Ear pieces Or ear spaces. The two small advertising spaces on the front page of a newspaper either side of the title or masthead.

Finished art Artwork. The final mechanical layout of type and pictures. (Often termed 'camera-ready', i.e. ready to be photographed and made into a plate before going to press.)

Finished artist The person responsible for preparing the above – usually under the direction of a designer.

Gate fold Any sheet of promotional literature folded twice across its width to form six pages.

Half-tone A photograph in print. The photograph is 'screened' or broken down into dots for lifelike reproduction.

Hard sell Hard-hitting advertising that pulls no verbal or visual punches. (The antithesis of 'soft sell'.)

Incentives   Promotional give-away to encourage the buying of a product, or to encourage sales-staff to put up a better performance. Anything from plastic daffodils and cassette tapes to staff participation schemes for exotic holidays.

Knock and drop   Leaflets or literature distributed door-to-door.

Launch   The start date of any given campaign – usually related to a new or revamped product.

Layout   A visualizer's scamp of how an ad will look on the printed page. Alternatively known as a 'rough' or a 'scribble'.

Logo   Logotype. The symbol or graphic device associated with a product, manufacturer or service company by which they can be identified.

Media   A generic term for the publications and broadcasting media within which advertising will appear.

Media schedule   A listing of the publications in which a campaign will appear. The schedule also includes dates of appearances and space costs.

Production   An all-embracing term for any mechanical work to be carried out to produce ads or printed material. Also, the agency department charged with the task of co-ordinating the various disciplines.

Promotion   Promo. Often the entire mix of advertising and below-the-line work for a given product. Also applied to a single competition or incentive.

Point-of-sale   Below-the-line sales material which is placed *in situ* with the product, e.g. on a shop counter.

Tag line   Or strap line. A line of copy, usually situated close to the logo, which sums up the quality of the product, or establishes the philosophy of the company. e.g. 'We'll take good care of you'.

Target audience   The socio-economic grouping with the wherewithal (income and intellectual motivation) to buy the product in question. Much work has been done to classify the various target groups and these are given ratings A to E. An A rating describes the top end of the market, while E denotes the lower income bracket.

Traffic 1   A term often used to identify potential customers who physically go to examine or try out a product – as in the 'traffic' through a car showroom, for instance.

Traffic 2   The agency department responsible for chasing work and seeing to it that material is produced on time.

USP   Unique selling proposition. The major benefit of a given product (goes faster, digs deeper, etc.) which establishes it as being better than a similar product made by a competitor.

Index